THE FIFTH TASTE . COOKING WITH UMAMI

THE
FIFTH
TASTE

COOKING WITH
UMAMI

DAVID KASABIAN & ANNA KASABIAN

UNIVERSE

FIRST PUBLISHED IN THE UNITED STATES OF AMERICA IN 2005
BY UNIVERSE PUBLISHING
A DIVISION OF RIZZOLI
INTERNATIONAL PUBLICATIONS, INC.
300 PARK AVENUE SOUTH
NEW YORK, NY 10010
WWW.RIZZOLIUSA.COM

2006 2007 2008 / 10 9 8 7 6 5 4 3 2

DISTRIBUTED IN THE U.S. TRADE BY RANDOM HOUSE, NEW YORK

PRINTED IN CHINA

DESIGNED : AISHA BURNES

ISBN : 0-7893-1356-1

LIBRARY OF CONGRESS CONTROL NUMBER : 2005905172

DEDICATION

For our mothers, aunts, and grandmothers, whose stoves and hearts were always warm for us, and who unknowingly in their Italian and Armenian kitchens taught us the joy of umami-packed food.

TABLE OF CONTENTS

FOREWORD

by MARK BITTMAN

By explaining umami—the seemingly mysterious, often misunderstood, yet completely essential and wonderful "fifth taste"—to American home cooks, Anna Kasabian and David Kasabian are doing something that should've been done a long time ago. And by combining their own recipes with those of some of the best and best-known food writers and chefs in the country, they're taking what would be a fascinating intellectual exploration and adding to it a great service, a collection of recipes, each of which is bound to explode with flavor.

Umami, as you're about to discover in these pages, is not only the fifth taste—salty, sweet, bitter, and sour are the first four—it's just as important as its far more famous predecessors, at least to cooks. That makes this an ambitious work—imagine, if you will, a book written about the flavor of "sweet," as if hundreds have not been done already—and one that, I imagine, will open a door that will in turn lead to a world of new cookbooks focused on umami.

That's something to look forward to, because just as people have sweet teeth, or people adore salty food, there are those of us who simply cannot get enough of umami. When I think of umami I think of some of my favorite ingredients: soy sauce, for example, and Parmesan—two of the greatest culinary inventions of the human race, and perfect examples of umami-packed foods. I also think of the closely related fish sauce (most commonly known by its Thai name, nam pla), which is ironic in a way because although the word *umami* is Japanese (just coined about a hundred years ago), the first example of a "recipe" producing umami is the fish sauce made by the ancient Greeks and Romans.

If you take fish sauce, or soy sauce, or any of a hundred other ingredients—from reduced chicken stock to dried mushrooms to ripe tomato—and add them to other foods, you boost their umami, which means, in short, you make them taste better. If you eat aged meat (or, for that matter, cheap cuts of meat) or well-made ham (like prosciutto), or "stinky" cheese, or miso soup, or if you drink good red wine, you're experiencing umami in a fairly pure form.

All of this, and much more, is lucidly explained by the Kasabians in the following pages, the first part of which is as exciting and intriguing a read as you'll find in any cookbook published this year. Halfway through the introduction, you'll know more about umami than all but a handful of people throughout the world did as recently as twenty years ago. If you follow their clever experiments in the opening chapter, you'll be able to identify not only umami but the four other tastes with more clarity and certainty than you ever did before.

Then there are the recipes. If umami is a good taste—and it is—what better than a cookbook that showcases it?

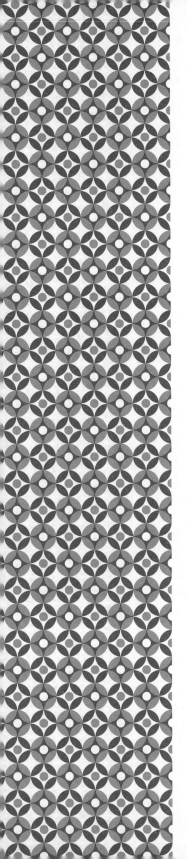

INTRODUCTION

In one sense, this book is something short of 3,000 years late. Records show that it was about that long ago that people in the Mediterranean began consciously adding umami to their food in the form of fermented fish sauce. This practice originated with the Greeks and was borrowed by the Romans, who variously called the condiment garum and liquamen. Of course, they did not know it was umami, but they did know that for some reason they apparently didn't ponder, it made just about everything they ate taste richer, meatier, more savory and satisfying. In a cookbook written by Marcus Apicius in the second century BCE, nearly every recipe calls for at least a splash or two of the stuff, sometimes a good deal more. Vast fortunes were made and grand cities built because of garum.

The first people who did ponder umami lived 1,200 years ago in what is now modern Japan. Here lighter fare of vegetables and fish made palates more sensitive to the presence of this subtle but satisfying taste. They too were unaware of exactly what gave rise to the umami taste they loved, but prodigious consumption of dashi broth, seafood, pickled vegetables, and later shoyu soy sauce—all rich in umami taste—attests to their grasp of umami's power to please.

It seems fitting then that the first umami substance identified would be in the lab of a Japanese scientist, Dr. Kikunae Ikeda, who in 1907 pointed to glutamate, an abundant amino acid, as the ingredient that he and generations of Japanese before him loved but could not identify. Acceptance of umami as a basic taste, distinct from sweet, sour, salty, and bitter, spread throughout Asia in the decades that followed. But it was not until the turn of our new millennium that umami was accepted as a true basic taste in the West. And that acceptance, and the understanding of how umami-rich ingredients can help us make better-tasting food—that can also be better for us—is really just beginning.

So in another sense, this book may be just in time. We have no doubt that the surge of interest in umami among Western cooks will gain momentum, and that the knowledge and understanding—both scientific and culinary—of how umami fits in our kitchens, on our tables, and in our appreciation of food, family, and friends, will grow rapidly as well.

We hope that this book can serve as more than a little shove to give that movement momentum, and become a useful guide to the joys of cooking and eating umami for the curious cooks among us.

PRESENTING A TASTE YOU ALREADY KNOW WELL: UMAMI

In just the past few years, the conscious use of umami (oo-MA-mee) in cooking has become a powerful new culinary force in America. Thousands of chefs and serious cooks have embraced it as an easy, healthy, and dramatic way to make food taste better by emphasizing umami's rich, meaty, savory qualities.

Along the way, some people have labeled umami a new taste, but it is clearly not new. No more than sweet, sour, salty, and bitter—the other four basic tastes—are new. Umami has always been there, we have always enjoyed it, we have even craved it, ever since humankind started to eat. Yet we, as Westerners anyway, just didn't know what it was—let alone what to call it—until recently.

It turns out that umami taste is one reason we adore tomatoes, corn, cheese, mushrooms, oysters, aged beef, and many other foods spanning cuisines of every culture on earth. These are all foods rich in umami taste. But, as much as umami might take credit for the enjoyment of a particular food, it is just one of many reasons we take pleasure in eating that food. The others include the balance among the other four tastes, the food's aroma, mouthfeel, and appearance, and even the sound it makes when you eat it. We'll investigate these in more detail later, but first some important definitions.

TASTE IS NOT FLAVOR

Some people use the terms taste and flavor interchangeably, as in "that vanilla ice cream tastes good," and "I like the salty flavor of clams." That's fine because that's the way normal people speak, yet taste and flavor have simple scientific distinctions that every cook can benefit greatly from understanding.

Tastes are sensations caused by compounds called *tastants*, as they enter your mouth, dissolve in saliva, and encounter chemical-sensing sites located on taste buds buried deep inside fungiform papillae on our tongues and elsewhere in the mouth.

When tastants such as sucrose (table sugar) and fructose (fruit sugars) hit the right taste buds, our brains register the sensation called sweet. With sodium chloride (table salt) hitting the right taste buds, we get the salty sensation. Acids are tastants in wine, vinegar, and lemon juice which we perceive as sour. And from alkaloids found in poisons like strychnine, household cleaners like ammonia, and from foods such as chocolate, coffee, tonic water, endive, and freshly ground black pepper, we taste bitter.

The other important chemical sense is aroma, which is what we smell of food. We acquire aroma from volatilized (i.e., vaporized) chemicals in our food called *odorants*. Odorants waft through our nostrils before food enters our mouths. They also rise through the opening behind the soft palate on the roof of the mouth as food is chewed or otherwise passes through. This is also where the enzymes in saliva dissolve and release newly developed odorants. Both passages lead to the olfactory receptors at the top of the nasal cavity, mere millimeters from the olfactory bulb on the brain where aroma signals are processed.

All taste buds taken together sense just five basic tastes (as far as we know). Olfactory receptors detect thousands of distinct aromas. The important principle is that *taste plus aroma equals what we call flavor*. In other words, taste happens in the mouth, aroma happens in the nasal cavity, and flavor happens when the two sensations meet in the brain (see The Taste-versus-Flavor Jelly Bean Test, page 25).

Most sensory experts regard a third sensation as a flavor component, and that is, irritation of the trigeminal nerve endings throughout the oral and nasal cavities. Stimulation of this nerve accounts for the pungent sensation when we eat things like chilis, horseradish, and raw garlic; the cool we get from alcohol and the menthol in mints, mouthwash, and some cigarettes; and the numbness inflicted by cloves, as well as the dentist's needle. Trigeminal stimulation is also the direct physical stimulation of the oral cavity from food temperatures and textures, and includes that titillating tingle of champagne bubbles on the tongue and roof of the mouth. This stimulation is often painful, but many people like it nonetheless (see The Factors of Food Enjoyment, page 20).

"TASTES GOOD, AND IT'S GOOD FOR YOU!"

It is a trite claim of bad advertising, but there's more than a tasty morsel of truth to it. Nearly all human sensations, including hunger, thirst, pleasure, pain, and so forth, are designed to help us survive and even thrive as individuals and as a species.

In the case of taste, it all sounds rather prehistoric considering our supposedly advanced state of civilization, but picture if you will a primitive ancestor of ours, unacquainted with principles of nutrition, foraging around for something to quell this hungry sensation about which he is equally ignorant. Fortunately, a taste mechanism has evolved in his mouth, nose, and brain to make sure he eats the good stuff and avoids the bad, most of the time anyway.

His acute taste for sweet ensures that he eats, among other things, foods rich in readily available carbohydrates, the fundamental fuel for his body. There's not that much really sweet tasting stuff for him to eat, so he probably walks around with an unsated sweet tooth, forever ready to eat his fill and beyond when he encounters that exhilarating taste. It is one he encounters strongly in ripe fruit and, to a lesser degree, in vegetables and meat.

His taste for salt might not be all that pleasing by itself. But salt enhances the taste of other foods like vegetables and nuts. So the salt he gets from fish, sea vegetables, animal blood, and salt deposits inspires him to eat a varied diet, all the while sneaking much needed minerals into his system. Once salt's importance was recognized by more advanced civilizations, it would go on to play a role of chief protagonist in cultures, economies, global exploration, religion, politics, and superstitions, all testaments to the magnitude of salt's human nutritional significance.

To our primal ancestor, bitter is distinctly unpleasant. Because most edibles in nature that would kill him taste bitter, like plant and animal poisons, this aversion helps him live to eat another day.

His ability to taste sour, which he also finds unpleasant, is a bit of a mystery. The simplest explanation for its existence may be that both unripe and decaying foodstuffs taste sour, signaling that it's not poison, but rather that it's either too soon or too late to be eating this particular substance. Theories abound.

For better or worse, we inherited this same taste mechanism, clearly designed for a less sophisticated and less prosperous generation of our species. We now enjoy a surplus of what used be scarce (sugar and salt), and have acquired tastes for what used to repel (bitter and sour). Sadly, too many of us are mindless slaves to our obsolete gustatory urges and constantly fill up on everything. The result is too much obesity, diabetes, hypertension, alcoholism, cardiovascular disease, cancer, and countless taste-manipulating food additives the unwary ingest daily.

But we can also thank our primitive taste faculty for our ability to make and eat some extraordinary food, if we are smart enough to transcend our impulses. And if we know what we're doing in the kitchen.

SO WHAT TASTES UMAMI?

Umami stands accused of being subtle and hard to describe. Granted, it is subtle, at least to many Westerners, but largely because we're not conscious of it the way we are conscious of, say, sweet and salty when we eat them. The Western diet is partly to blame since it tends toward fattier, more highly flavored foods that compete with umami and diminish the impression it makes. Asians, particularly Japanese eating a more traditional diet, recognize the umami in an oyster as instinctively as Westerners recognize the salt. Nonetheless, umami works it magic with less overt effect.

Umami, however, is not hard to describe—no harder, really, than describing sweet, sour, salty, or bitter. Among the most apt descriptors are savory, mouth-filling, brothy, meaty, satisfying, and rich. Like salt, it isn't all that pleasant by itself, but it makes other foods taste much better, sometimes turning the nearly unpalatable into a rewarding feast. Umami extends the finish of savory foods, making them linger on the palate longer. It also alters our perception of other tastes, making salt saltier, sweet sweeter, and bitter and sour less biting. We have included some taste tests to help you zero in on the umami taste so you'll know it when you taste it.

We get umami taste from many food-borne substances. A misconception that persists to this day holds that the singular source of umami is glutamic acid or glutamate*, an amino acid found in varying concentrations in just about everything we eat, both animal and vegetable. Glutamate is the most abundant amino acid in nature. It is also the star ingredient in monosodium glutamate, or MSG. But don't draw conclusions about that fact just yet. A more detailed discussion follows.

Like many other amino acids, glutamate has numerous roles in the body. In fact, glutamate isn't just the most abundant amino acid, it is also the busiest, performing more functions in the human body than any other single amino acid. One job is as a

---

* Glutamic acid is the proper name of the amino acid under discussion, while glutamate denotes a compound (usually a salt, e.g., monosodium glutamate) with glutamic acid as a major component. To a scientist, this a big deal. To a cook, this distinction makes little difference since they both taste the same. In the interest of simplicity and with apologies to sticklers (whom we deeply admire) we use the terms synonymously.

neural transmitter, aiding the flow of information around in our brains. Another is as a building block of proteins, which are chains of amino acids, sometimes hundreds of molecules long. Depending on which amino acids they are made of and how they are arranged, different proteins are suited to different functions in the body. Some become muscle tissue, others go on to become enzymes, still others form brain cells, and so forth. Human life requires upward of 100,000 different proteins, each with a unique composition and characteristics.

Glutamate is called a nonessential amino acid because our bodies can fabricate all the glutamate we need, meaning it is not essential that we get it from our diets (in spite of the fact that we eat plenty of it anyway). Of the twenty amino acids used in our bodies for constructing proteins, there are nine we can't manufacture ourselves. These are called essential amino acids because it is essential to include them in our diets or we risk protein deficiency. Inattentive vegans are at risk for this because some essential amino acids, notably methionine and lysine, are lacking in some legumes and grains. It's important to note that in order for glutamate to have umami taste it must be in a free state, in other words, not bound up as part of a protein molecule (see page 24). But science is just learning what umami-enlightened cooks have known all along, which is that glutamate isn't the only umami-tasting substance that we eat. Far from it.

PROFESSOR FINDS UMAMI IN BOWL OF SOUP

One day in 1907, Dr. Kikunae Ikeda, a gifted 44-year-old chemistry professor at the Imperial Tokyo University, sat down to a bowl of soup.

As he ate, his thoughts turned again to his persistent notion that this soup, made with a traditional Japanese broth of kombu sea vegetable and dried bonito tuna, had a taste unlike any other. This taste wasn't sweet or sour, salty or bitter. Instead, Dr. Ikeda thought of it as savory, rich, meaty, and especially satisfying. It was a taste that he could not duplicate with any combination of other tastes. This was something different.

Dr. Ikeda followed his hunch and set to work in the lab where, after considerable experimentation and persistence, he isolated from kombu a substance responsible for this taste. What he found was the amino acid glutamate. Glutamate was discovered in 1866 by Dr. Karl Ritthausen, a German chemist studying wheat proteins. (It was named by Dr. Ritthausen after wheat's most famous protein, gluten; he found plentiful amounts of glutamate within wheat gluten.) It appears from scientific records that Dr. Ritthausen did not eat any of his glutamate, or if he did, it did not impress him as a distinct taste. But thanks to Ritthausen's work forty years earlier, Ikeda knew exactly what he had found.

Eager to name the newly identified taste, Ikeda took the suggestion of an associate and labeled it *umami*, but only until a better name came along. It never did. Umami is the name that stuck. Umami is a Japanese word which by Ikeda's time had been used for at least a century to denote that quality of a food that is especially pleasing, or an especially good example of what a particular food should taste like: the perfect vegetable, the perfect shellfish, the perfect sake. In Japanese, *umai* means delicious, and *mi* means essence. To this day, many Japanese call any food that reaches a state of perfection *umami*, without particular regard for its free glutamate content.

Initially, Ikeda extracted a mere 30 grams of glutamate from 12 kilograms of kombu, thereby inventing MSG, or monosodium glutamate, a stable and water-soluble salt of glutamic acid. In doing so, he also launched an industry that would change food forever.

Using Dr. Ikeda's patent, a company now called Ajinomoto (roughly translated as "Instant Taste") was established to manufacture and market MSG. The product was a hit almost immediately, first in Japan, then across Asia. By the 1930s and 1940s, it had spread throughout most of Europe and North America, although it was never embraced in the West as earnestly as it was in the East.

We have Dr. Ikeda to thank for many things, but especially for awakening the world to the fact that the umami sensation is real, distinct, and worthy of every cook's attention. Unfortunately, in the minds of many, umami and MSG are one. If you use MSG, you taste umami, if you taste umami, there must certainly be MSG, or so it goes. This overly narrow definition was established, no doubt, because the spontaneous and widespread success of MSG in Asia as the umami-maker-in-a-shaker caused the two identities to meld. Too bad.

Just a few years after Ikeda's MSG breakthrough, further lab work by Ikeda's disciple Dr. Shintaro Kodama revealed another powerful source of umami taste. He identified it as a nucleotide called inosine monophosphate (also known as IMP) which he found in katsuobushi, the dried bonito tuna flakes in Ikeda's soup. A nucleotide is a compound fundamental to the fabric of RNA and DNA, the most basic genetic materials, and is distinct from amino acids such as glutamate. More importantly, Kodama found that

---

DR. IKEDA'S SOUP

Nobody knows precisely which soup Dr. Ikeda ate before making the glutamate/umami connection, but most agree it was probably *dashi*, a stock as basic to Japanese cuisine as veal stock is to French.

This recipe is for a basic dashi which gets its intense umami from kombu, a type of sea vegetable, with synergy from katsuobushi, flakes of dried bonito tuna (see Sources, page 194). Make this soup at home, or go to a good Japanese restaurant and order it. It's worth eating because it tastes so good, and because it is, after all, not just a recipe but a leading player in umami history.

ICHIBAN DASHI

Do not let this boil. It will turn murky and slimy.

SERVES 4

½ ounce **kombu** sea vegetable (about 20 square inches)

5 cups cold spring water

½ cup dried **bonito flakes** (katsuobushi), packed tightly

1. Wipe the kombu clean with a dry cloth. Do not wash it; the white powder on the leaves is natural glutamate.
2. Soak the kombu in the cooking water for 1 hour or more.
3. Cook gently over medium heat to just below boiling.
4. Turn off heat, add the bonito flakes, stir once, and cover for 2 minutes, until the bonito settles to the bottom. Skim if necessary.
5. Strain through cheesecloth or very fine strainer.
6. Eat as is, or add cooked noodles and vegetables.

*Ingredients contributing significant umami appear in **boldface type**.

a little bit of this nucleotide dramatically amplified the umami intensity of glutamate, a quality called synergy, a hallmark of umami taste.

From the 1950s through the 1970s, more umami-triggering and umami-synergizing nucleotides were discovered, including guanosine monophosphate (GMP), adenosine monophosphate (AMP), and xanthosine monophosphate (XMP). By the 1990s, researchers were finding one umami substance after another. In 1998, Yamaguchi and Ninomiya, two leading umami researchers, published a list of thirty-nine substances they believed trigger umami. These included other amino acids, as well as ibotenic and tricolomic acids, both found in some mushrooms; succinic acid which is plentiful in sake, shellfish, and wine; theanine, a taste component of tea; and an octopeptide (compound of eight amino acids) found in beef broth, dubbed BMP for "beefy, meaty peptide."

Clearly, glutamate is part of but not nearly the entire story of umami. It would take a few more years and some scientific breakthroughs before the picture came into focus.

THE ENIGMA (AND STIGMA) OF MSG

From the start, MSG won little respect in the West. Dr. Ikeda's 1912 speech to the Eighth International Congress of Applied Chemistry in New York, extolling MSG, reportedly inspired more nap-taking than note-taking.

From the time Ikeda introduced it in 1908, MSG established itself swiftly in kitchens and on tables nearly everywhere in Asia. Yet, in the first half of the twentieth century, MSG had just two tiny toe-holds in the West. One was in Asian communities, where MSG was used in the home and in restaurants open to the occidental public. The second was as a mostly experimental additive in a few small-scale industrial food preparations, a practice that didn't grow much until after World War II. GIs returning from the Pacific Theater had eaten MSG, and liked it. This set off a boom in the Chinese restaurant business, aided the growing food-manufacturing industry, and spawned creation of MSG seasonings, notably Ac'cent, which endures to this day.

In 1968, a Chinese-born American doctor named Robert Ho Man Kwok wrote to the *New England Journal of Medicine* asking if readers could help figure out why he and his friends suffered dizziness, headaches, and numbness shortly after eating in certain Chinese restaurants. His letter was published, conjectures poured in, and the Chinese Restaurant Syndrome debate ignited.

Dr. Kwok himself named MSG as a leading suspect, but not until a year later was MSG convicted, and not of one crime, but two. The most damning evidence was put forth in two unrelated studies appearing in a single 1969 issue of the magazine *Science*. In one, Dr. Herbert Shaumberg of the Albert Einstein School of Medicine, argued a convincing case that MSG caused Chinese Restaurant Syndrome symptoms, a position he formerly scorned. But worse than that was a study by Dr. John Olney of Washington University, asserting that rats injected with MSG suffered brain damage. More studies followed and more MSG indictments were handed down alleging numerous debilitating and fatal conditions. In most of these studies, rodent subjects were injected with massive doses of MSG, many times more than they (or we humans) could ever get into the bloodstream through ingestion. Needless to say, the rats got sick, and MSG took the rap.

Further studies aimed at connecting MSG to Chinese Restaurant Syndrome never produced anything like Dr. Shaumberg's results—at least not those studies conducted with rigorous, double-blind techniques, a practice necessary to avoid derision from the serious scientific community. Every study undertaken in the proper fashion supports the view that MSG is perfectly safe and mostly symptom-free for the vast majority of people eating reasonably normal diets.

An equal or greater number of reliable studies also show that people actually prefer food with MSG, at sensible levels, making it a worthwhile tool for nutritionists. MSG is quite successful in sparking the deadened appetites of the aged, the ailing, and children with certain eating disorders. MSG contains less than a third the sodium of table salt, yet even a small amount amplifies the perception of salt (see The Umami–versus–Salt Taste Test, page 31), so it is convenient in reduced-sodium diets. And because it helps create satiety, recipes with a little MSG can avoid much fat and still please.

Yet to this day, detractors insist that adding MSG to foods sets off a frightening number of human maladies, including brain lesions, Alzheimer's, Parkinson's, ALS (Lou Gehrig's disease), Huntington's chorea, and sexual dysfunction in the offspring of glutamate-eating women. And this, they claim, is in addition to the annoying but doubtlessly more benign headaches, dizziness, chest pains, bloating, burning, flushing, fatigue, insomnia, joint pain, diarrhea, vomiting, numbness, tremors, skin rash, rapid heartbeat, asthma, runny nose, insomnia, and general weakness, all pinned on MSG.

How can one little molecule with just nineteen atoms inflict so many and so varied a set of symptoms? One theory proposes that glutamate is not just a neurotransmitter but also a neurotoxin that kills brain cells by overexciting them when concentrations are too high—sort of an anatomical role reversal in which the brain actually causes physical ills rather than dutifully detecting and dealing with them. This theory is refuted by science showing that dietary glutamate never makes it to the brain and that the brain makes all the glutamate it needs by itself, thank you very much.

Some people are so convinced of MSG's toxicity they urge avoidance of all glutamate, even that delivered in our diets through natural foods, most of which contain at least some free glutamate. This goal seems difficult if not unattainable, and in clear conflict with our instinctual craving for the glutamate abundant in natural food.

The United States Food and Drug Administration (FDA) has not been silent on the subject. They have devoted serious resources to the study of MSG's safety in food, and have frequently and consistently concluded it is harmless. In 1959, the FDA granted MSG its Generally Recognized As Safe (GRAS) status, the most lenient category for any food substance and one that includes salt, baking soda, and vinegar. They concurred several times more, backed by scrupulous studies through the 1970s and '80s. They did so again in 1995 when they embraced conclusions drawn in the landmark Federation of American Societies for Experimental Biology (FASEB) report showing that MSG is safe for everyone, save for a minute percentage of the population who may suffer a small number of minor, inconsequential symptoms.

Meanwhile, food manufacturers continue to use MSG (known as E621 in the food-additive world) in concentrations they call similar to those found in nature, and do so in hundreds of prepared foods including salad dressings, soups, sauces, spice mixes, ice cream, cookies, chewing gum, frozen meals, and all manner of reduced-fat and reduced-salt products. The reasons are, as expected, economic. MSG makes food taste better to the general public so people eat more of it. And some food manufacturers help control costs by using MSG instead of higher-quality ingredients. Salt and sugar are, of course, employed in similar culinary misdeeds.

Nonetheless, the FDA requires that foods to which MSG has been added be clearly labeled as such. That regulation rather narrowly covers the use of a white powdery substance composed of 78% free glutamic acid, 21% sodium, and 1% contaminants that we find, for example, in a package of Ac'cent. But it does not cover other glutamate-bearing substances innocently appearing on ingredient lists on hundreds of packaged foods. Although the FDA acknowledges the need to correct the apparent deception, even foods that proclaim "No MSG" or "No Added MSG" on their labels might contain textured protein, hydrolyzed protein, monopotassium glutamate, sodium caseinate, calcium caseinate, yeast food, hydrolyzed yeast, autolyzed yeast, or yeast extract. These are just some of the euphemisms for what is, in fact, glutamate. Some would say that the public's widespread distrust of MSG has deeply moved food makers—not to take glutamate out of their food, but to find ways of delivering it under unassuming pseudonyms.

That said, our research has not uncovered a single report of similar symptoms from eating any quantity, no matter how absurdly huge, of ripe red tomatoes, Parmesan cheese, soy sauce, or any other glutamate-loaded food. Furthermore, sensory testing conducted by both the glutamate industry and independent laboratories consistently shows that once certain levels of added MSG are reached, palatability plummets. Too much MSG makes food taste bad. No such parallel exists with foods naturally rich in glutamates. The more glutamates are packed into natural foods, the better they taste, up to a point of taste saturation. But natural glutamate never tastes bad.

It seems from this that natural glutamates are fundamentally different from MSG, perhaps as the natural sweetness of a ripe, just-picked strawberry is worlds away from refined sugar.

We have two messages about MSG. First, there's probably nothing to fear, really. Second, why bother? If you're looking for umami, why not go for the real thing in quality unprocessed foods? There are plenty to be had, and MSG is, after all, an industrially produced chemical, bereft of the myriad other tastes, aromas, nutrients, sights, smiles, memories, and other satisfying sensations that natural umami transports along with it.

THIS BUD'S FOR UMAMI

By the end of the twentieth century, umami had been the subject of sufficiently intense scrutiny that most scientists, if pressed, would say that umami probably is a distinct basic taste. But then again, maybe not. After all, until then, most of the evidence had come from research of a sensory nature, relying on people sipping standardized lab-made samples and reporting what they thought they could taste, or on everyday lab mice expressing their preferences by drinking one sample and not another. It is a methodology that is quite rigorous and widely respected, but nonetheless, some allege, subject to errors in human judgment and observation. Although convincing to many, this sort of evidence raises eyebrows among the hardnosed, show-me-an-electrical-signal-going-to-the-brain-and-I'll-believe-you school of scientists.

Suddenly, in January 2000, the foundation for lingering doubt began to crumble when a team of researchers at the University of Miami reported they had zeroed in on the umami taste bud. Technically speaking, they identified a G-protein-coupled receptor on a mouse tongue they named "taste-mGluR4." It contains a molecule shaped perfectly for bonding with a complementarily-shaped amino acid molecule. When this happens, taste-mGluR4 chemically arouses the taste bud, an electrical signal goes off to the brain, and the brain says, "Mmm, umami."

This discovery is significant to everyone who eats. By showing that umami is a genuine basic taste, it proves that the umami we love can't be had any other way. You must eat umami-rich food, period. More importantly, it says we had better take umami in our food seriously, for it's not just enjoyable, it's part of an overall design to keep us alive.

Unlike other eating sensations, tastes are biological imperatives. They are the last line of defense against poisons. And they are the indispensable custodians of our dietary well-being, identifying and measuring basic nutrients as we take them in.

Aromas, by contrast, may be something we like, something our appetites might be triggered by, but they tell us little about the nutritive value of foods. Smelling roasted meat or fragrant fruit may bring us great and satisfying pleasure, but we can easily sustain life without the aroma of roasts, fruit, or anything else. We cannot, however, live without salt, carbohydrates, or, apparently, umami. To ensure compliance with this simple law of nature, our brains reward us with extra delight when we gratify our tastes, and refuse to signal satisfaction until we do. Taste is an itch that must be scratched.

From this it seems that taste, not aroma, might be judged the principal sensation of eating. If so, then a great cook is one who strives for balance and expression among all the senses, recognizing that skillful use of tastes—umami among them—does the most to make eaters happy, and healthy.

HOW DO I LOVE UMAMI? LET ME COUNT THE WAYS

Scientists lament that taste is the least-understood sense, but in the past, their tools and knowledge base allowed for little more than informed guesses about how taste works. In the last fifteen years, technology has changed that. We now live in a world of sophisticated computers, cloned cells, transgenic mice (sort of designer lab animals with genetic profiles made to order), and exquisitely sensitive instruments that measure almost infinitesimally small biological signals. A torrent of brilliant new discoveries in taste science has just begun.

While far from complete, the emerging picture of umami taste mechanics might not surprise an observant eater. The umami taste receptors (their identities since refined as proteins labeled T1R1 and T1R3) respond very strongly to glutamate, as expected, but also to nearly every other amino acid to varying degrees. We now know not to say that umami is the taste of glutamate or MSG. That's way too narrow. Instead, umami is turning out to be the broadly tuned taste of many amino acids—essential, nonessential, and non-protein-building alike. It also looks like the entire array of umami-triggering amino acids is subject to the striking synergizing effect of nucleotides such as IMP, GMP, AMP, and XMP, among others. Eat a little GMP (plentiful in shiitake mushrooms) along with your amino acids, and hold on for an umami kick.

Finally, inquisitive cooks can stop scratching their heads, wondering how the glorious, even thrilling effect of umami could possibly be caused by one simple chemical. It is not. Glutamate is but a single note played by a lone instrument. Real umami can be anything from a piano solo to a jazz band to an entire symphony orchestra playing luscious chords and flowing melodies of intertwining instruments and rhythms, as the chefs' recipes that follow demonstrate.

The principal reason we love umami may be straightforward: Our brains like it when we give our bodies food that's easy to use. Complete proteins are not easy to use (nor do they have much taste, incidentally). Before we can do anything with them, complete proteins must be broken down into their amino acid components through digestion. This demands energy (which is one of the reasons people doze off after a big meal). Umami is the taste of amino acids that are ready for our bodies to use. The well-known restorative effects of chicken soup, laden with an assortment of amino acids, bears testament to that.

It also makes sense that we are more highly tuned for glutamate, a plentiful nonessential amino acid, because it is the main source of the fuel our intestines use to digest everything else.

The dietary motive for the synergizing effect of nucleotides remains more mysterious. It has long been held that dietary intake of nucleotides, whether for building DNA and RNA or for their vital role in metabolism, is unnecessary since our cells do a great job of salvaging and reusing these materials when spent. However, a growing body of science shows that dietary nucleotides are key to building a healthy immune system in the young (mother's milk is loaded with the stuff) and maintaining it in adulthood.

So it seems our unconscious psychological yearning for umami actually supports a complex system of biological needs. We seek amino acids for protein-building, for use as metabolic fuel, and for many other crucial functions, and we hit the umami jackpot when we mix them with nucleotides, vital to battling disease. The great assortment of umami triggers and synergizers

5. FOOD APPEARANCE—Are the colors appetizing (red tomatoes, green broccoli, deeply seared scallops)? Does it look moist or dry? Is it placed artfully on a plate or slopped on? Is there a lot of it or just a delicate, tantalizing morsel?

6. AROMA—Hot food typically exudes aromas we sense before we eat, both while the food is cooking and when we're about to dig in. That's less true with cold foods, which need to be warmed in our mouths before they exhibit aroma. In both cases aroma goes on to play a central role in eating delight.

7. TASTE—Once we bite into food, we soon detect whether it is sweet, sour, salty, bitter, or umami, the sensations we get in our mouths. Tastes trigger salivation, an event that starts the process of digestion in the mouth, helps release odorants to be sensed in the olfactory, and dilutes and delivers tastants to the taste buds. Aroma works together with taste to create what we call flavor. Some tastes and flavors strike us the moment they enter our mouths. Others, particularly fat-soluble flavors, take a little longer to make themselves known. Still others are created by the enzyme action of saliva and don't develop until later, sometimes well after a bite is chewed and swallowed.

8. TEMPERATURE—Is the food hot or cold, or a combination of both? In general, we like soups hot, salads cold, and red wine, cheese, and leftover pizza at room temperature.

9. ASTRINGENCY—Some substances, like the tannins in red wine, bind with proteins and complex sugars in saliva, robbing it of viscosity. This not only makes the oral cavity less slippery, it has the added effect of amplifying all five tastes, as well as heat from chilis, black pepper, ginger, and garlic.

Continued

See Spicy, below. A bit of astringency can refresh the mouth (as does sourness), letting us taste successive bites with a cleansed palate—a job the acid in wine does very well.

10. TEXTURE—Is the food soft, brittle, tender, grainy, smooth, dry, oily? As food rubs around the inside of your mouth, its texture is revealed. We seem to enjoy every texture, but not with every food. Mashed potatoes should be soft; a potato chip should not. The culinary term for texture is mouthfeel.

11. SPICY—Some people think of heat from chilis and onions as a taste. It isn't, but is instead a chemical irritation of mouth tissue. The capsaicin in chilis, piperine in black pepper, gingerol in ginger, and isothiocyanates in garlic and onions are actually doing damage and causing minor pain, but many people like it anyway.

12. OTHER TRIGEMINAL STIMULATION— There is a rather large nerve complex running through our faces called the trigeminal, and it is responsible for all kinds of oral sensations, including temperature, texture, spiciness, and menthol coolness, as described on page 11. There's one other trigeminal nerve stimulation that people experience which comes from beverage carbonation. Sip a soda or Champagne and take note of the assault on your tongue and soft palate. Some people don't like some of these trigeminal stimulations, others crave them like drugs.

13. CHEWING—Your mother was right: Chew your food well, because the very act of chewing helps create satisfaction (hence the abundant gum-chewing among those trying to quit smoking).

14. SOUND—Sometimes, we like to hear our food, too: The sizzle of grilling, the cracking of a lobster shell, the subtle slurp of eating an oyster, the distinct crunch of

Continued

invites us to eat a varied and interesting diet with infinite combinations of meats, fruits, and vegetables, predisposing us to complete and balanced diets. The most pleasing combinations, the ones with the best aromas, textures, and tastes (including the most delectably and healthfully synergized umami) become favorite recipes, to be enjoyed time and again.

What a wonderfully harmonious system this is!

AND THEN ALONG CAME KOKUMI

We thank the people of Japan and their sensitivity to subtleties in food qualities for revealing the existence of umami, and for generously lending us their word. It appears more thanks may be in order for teaching us about yet another food quality called *kokumi*, a nascent culinary buzzword now on the tips of every five taste–sensing tongue in the manufactured-food world, and maybe soon among chefs, depending on what it turns out to really mean.

Taste–enhancement makers including Ajinomoto and Kyowa Hakko are touting kokumi additives they say are not umami, but still create taste sensations of thickness, "mouthfulness," and continuity. Kokumi is said to have tremendous impact (meaning it is sensed immediately upon entering the mouth), to increase enjoyment of other foods, and to linger pleasantly on the palate, encouraging satiety. One company credits their product with delivering a roast meat flavor. Sounds an awful lot like umami to us. A peek behind the curtain reveals much.

In a report published in *Agricultural Food Chemistry* in 2003, a German team describes Kokumi substances that constitute "a new class of umami-type taste compound" produced from "glyco-conjugates of glutamic acid" produced using "Maillard-mimetic approaches." Bingo! We know about Maillard. The Maillard (pronounced "my-ARD") reaction is fundamental to so much good cooking, it bears explanation.

When we brown protein-rich foods, that is, grill a steak, sear a chicken breast, roast coffee, or bake bread until its crust is golden brown, most people refer to that as caramelizing—but it is not. Caramelizing is the product of ordinarily colorless and odorless sugars heated to temperatures at which they break down and re-form into hundreds of compounds, with sour and bitter tastes in addition to sweet, as well as numerous complex aromas. This happens, for example, when sugar-bearing vegetables such as onions and garlic are sautéed, and when confectioners turn out caramel candy. Depending on the sugar, caramelization takes place between 240 degrees F (for fructose) and 338 degrees F (for sucrose, or table sugar).

On the other hand, the Maillard reaction (named for the French physician Louis Camille Maillard, who figured all this out about the same time Dr. Ikeda was inventing MSG) requires amino acids in addition to sugars. The Maillard reaction takes place with considerably less heat, too: nominally 250 degrees F if searing meat or toasting bread. But it can, and does, occur at much cooler temperatures when brewing beer, aging balsamic vinegar, braising a roast, or reducing stock to a demi-glace; all are beneficiaries of Maillard's taste-, aroma-, and color-enriching transformations.

Because amino acids are present in the Maillard reaction, foods thus prepared exhibit a richer, more complex character compared to those prepared using caramelization. And if you have ever endured a pork chop not properly browned or pale-crusted bread retrieved from the oven too soon, you know how important Maillard is to eating pleasure. The Maillard reaction is also responsible for the sticky brown stuff left behind in the pan after searing meat. French chefs call this *fond*, or foundation, and foundation it is for luxurious sauces with deep, rich character and . . . well, lots of umami.

Which brings us back to kokumi. Is it really something apart from umami, as the food-additive makers say? Or is really just a newly discovered dimension of umami? It would not be the first time such a discovery happened. And could it be that kokumi additives are also a way for food manufacturers to deliver umami-enhancing chemicals without MSG, still much maligned and still, in the minds of many, synonymous with umami? We shall see. But in the meantime, we count anything with enhanced impact, mouthfulness, and continuity involving amino acids as part of the amazingly complex umami fabric. But it is still too soon to know for sure.

chewing stir-fried vegetables or a potato chip. But sometimes we don't: The sound made by biting down on sand in our salad, for example, is most unwelcome.

15. FINISH—How long do the tastes, aromas, and other qualities linger? How do they change over time? Finish has long been regarded as a key factor when evaluating wines, but it is equally important when we evaluate food. A long finish that matures and transforms in your mouth and nose is food you can savor between bites, and even after the last bite is gone. Good food with a long finish is the most satisfying food you can eat.

16. SATIETY—Pleasurable as it may be, eating is a biology-driven behavior that ensures sufficient fuel and bodily-maintenance materials. And our bodies have a way of letting us know if we've eaten enough of what it needs. Satiety is that feeling of contentment and fulfillment we get, including that sense of warmth in the tummy, especially when a meal is excellent in every regard.

CRAB À LA LAB

In a perverse demonstration of just how far food science has come, Japanese researchers reproduced the characteristic taste of snow crab from various chemicals, including amino acids and nucleotides. No crabs were harmed in the process, because there weren't any actual crabs used. Here is the recipe.

GLYCINE

ALANINE

ARGININE

MSG

IMP

SALT

Mix thoroughly and serve. Or not.

COOKING WITH UMAMI

Everything we eat with so much as a trace of protein and genetic material has some umami. Whether it is in a concentration or form sufficient for us to enjoy is a matter of nature's endowment and the method of preparation we employ.

There are two fundamental forms of umami the cook will do well to understand, as they influence the taste of a dish in different ways.

First is what we call *basic umami*, delivered by amino acids, the building blocks of proteins. Much, but by no means all, basic umami taste comes from glutamic acid, the most abundant amino acid in nature. The rest comes from other amino acids and some peptides, which are chains of amino acids just a few molecules long. In order for these amino acids to taste umami they must be in a free state; in other words, not bound up in a protein molecule.

Some foods are rich in these free amino acids when they are harvested and have a lot of umami taste when raw. Generally, the more mature the food, the higher the level of free amino acids. Other foods may have bound amino acids which, if they are to contribute umami taste, must be freed from their protein molecules, thus developing umami taste. There are two ways to do this.

The first is cooking, including kokumi-style searing, during which the agitating action of heat breaks down proteins into amino acids with the basic umami taste, as well as other umami compounds. The second way is to allow enzymes, both natural and those produced by microbes, to go about their jobs as demolition experts, ripping proteins apart into their tasty amino acid components. Aging beef, making cheese, fermenting beer, and letting dough rise slowly are all examples of enzymatic actions that help liberate basic umami.

Even food naturally high in basic umami may be cooked or fermented for other reasons, such as preservation, palatability, or digestibility. On the other hand, some foods lacking in naturally free amino acids will not tolerate such harsh treatment and will never taste umami.

The second form is what we call *synergizing umami*, delivered by nucleotides, building blocks of DNA and RNA, nature's most basic genetic materials. They go by names like IMP, GMP, AMP, and XMP, and are found in abundance in meats, shellfish, and mushrooms. They too may be in a free form or bound up in larger, tasteless molecules. Like basic umami, synergizing umami is developed when these large molecules are broken down into their tasty free nucleotide forms by cooking and enzymatic action. We call these synergizing umami because both research and everyday experience have shown that when synergizing umami is eaten along with basic umami, the umami sensation is multiplied, sometimes by many factors.

Knowing which foods contain which kind of umami (many foods have both) and what state it is in can help you make meals that are more delicious, or at least know when it's the umami in the food that's making you giddy.

UMAMI INGREDIENTS

The following description of food categories and their umami content is surely incomplete, maybe too rigid, scientifically debatable, and perhaps tainted with the occasional outright error. It is made even less reliable by the differences in umaminess from one specimen of a food to the next, especially when they differ in age, freshness, terroir, and seasonality, among many other aspects. Nonetheless we hope the following section serves as a useful guide to what is undoubtedly a rapidly evolving state of the umami culinary art.

GARDEN VEGETABLES AND FRUITS

Some garden vegetables are high in basic umami when raw, particularly, it seems, those allowed to mature more fully before harvesting. These include corn (which is technically a grain), peas, and other legumes, as well as tomatoes, mature potatoes, red bell peppers, winter squashes, walnuts, almonds, and sunflower seeds.

THE TASTE–VERSUS–FLAVOR JELLY BEAN TEST

This test works with nearly any food but is especially instructive using Jelly Belly or other authentically flavored jelly beans. It is designed to demonstrate the difference between taste—sensations that start on your tongue—and flavor—the combination of taste with aroma, which is picked up by the olfactory sensors at the top of your nasal cavity.

1. With eyes closed, remove one jelly bean from the bag.

2. Hold your nose, don't look, and put the jelly bean in your mouth and chew for 10 seconds.

3. What do you taste? Probably just sweet and maybe a touch of sour or salt, depending on the jelly bean you chose.

4. Release your nostrils and breath. Now what do you get? A blast of watermelon, strawberry, licorice, chocolate pudding, bubblegum, popcorn, or whatever flavor jelly bean you just ate, because your olfactory receptors can now get the aroma.

5. Make a mental note of the experience, and try it again with other jelly beans, and then with other foods. Pay attention to the sweet, sour, and salty sensations, and then the aromas. Soon the difference between taste and aroma will be ingrained, and you will have mastered the concept of flavor. It's not hard.

The basic umami of less-mature plant foods sometimes benefits from a little coaxing through cooking or fermentation. Green beans, new potatoes, carrots, asparagus, brussels sprouts, cabbages, and many cooking greens such as kale and Swiss chard are among them. However, some of these will never achieve the basic umami levels of the ripe varieties mentioned above unless cooked beyond palatability—and then what's the point?

Little can be done to improve umami in celery, cucumbers, zucchini, green tomatoes, most baby vegetables, or lettuce. However, like most foods, they taste better when umami foods are eaten with them, hence the ubiquitous tomato in your salad and dressings made with cheese and anchovies.

Synergizing umami is found in asparagus, spinach, potatoes, and many legumes including lima beans, kidney beans, navy beans, lentils, and peas, usually brought about by cooking.

Fresh fruits, no matter how mature, have very little umami, either basic or synergizing.

SEA VEGETABLES

Sea vegetables are an especially concentrated source of basic umami—obvious, of course, when we recall that Dr. Ikeda discovered glutamate in dashi, a soup based on sea vegetables. Kombu, arame, wakame, dulce, nori, laver, alaria, kelp, and others are among the many names of what Westerners once disdainfully miscalled seaweeds. In addition to their superb basic umami content, they are also excellent sources of minerals, including iron and calcium.

Most are typically purchased dried, although they are increasingly available fresh from sea vegetable farms. If dried, resist the urge to wash off the white powder that often accumulates on the leaves and fronds. That is pure, natural glutamate.

There is some synergizing umami in sea vegetables, especially laver, which is used to make the nori wrapped around your sushi hand roll.

MEATS AND POULTRY

Overall, meats and poultry have both basic and synergizing umami, although the amounts vary widely.

As with garden vegetables, maturity seems to be a key to umami in meat products. For example, a young Cornish game hen, which is tender and sweet, has less naturally occurring umami than a tough old fowl. The former tastes best if seared well at the start of cooking to develop umami among other flavor components. The later does fine tossed in a pot with water and boiled. And because it must cook longer, the fowl will develop far more synergizing umami than its young cousin will ever get the chance to do.

Among poultry, duck is quite high in both basic and synergizing umami, but less so in a rare-cooked breast than a long-braised confit of duck leg. But it is turkey, cooked in any number of ways, that tops the umami chart for poultry.

Surprising to some, beef has a relatively low basic umami compared to poultry. Once again, the tougher beef cuts—brisket, shanks, chuck, and such—have the most, and because they are often braised, the umami content is elevated during preparation. All cuts of beef are improved with dry aging, a process that allows naturally occurring enzymes to break down some of the flesh, enhancing tenderness, umami, and overall flavor. Thorough searing of all beef cuts is important to umami and total flavor, but is imperative for naturally tender cuts, which will taste shallow and one dimensional if this is not done to the proper degree. Lamb is similar to beef in these regards.

In assessing basic umami, we see that pork is like beef, but it packs far more synergizing umami, which means a little goes a long way when eaten with basic umami foods. Cured pork products, such as bacon and everyday cured hams, are even more intense, while premium cured hams such as Italian prosciutto, Spanish serrano, and American Smithfield are among the umami-rich treasures of the culinary world. Other cured meats, including sausage, jerky, and even some cold cuts, boast elevated umami levels. However, fresh sausages (like Italian sausages, Mexican chorizo, knockwurst, and haggis) are not cured, and when cooked develop only as much umami as the meats they are made from.

Impressive levels of synergizing umami are also supplied in veal and venison, no matter how they are cooked or otherwise made ready for the table.

In all animals, the densest concentrations of synergizing umami are organ meats or offal, although they usually contain far more cholesterol, which calls their dietary appeal into question.

Broths and stocks made from the meat and bones of all these animals pack prodigious umami wallop, especially those simmered long and slowly, releasing a wide assortment of amino acids and nucleotides in elevated concentrations.

DAIRY AND CHEESES

Straight from the udder, cow's milk has little umami of any kind (in contrast to human milk which is loaded with both kinds of umami), but depending on the journey it takes afterward, that assessment may change.

Buttermilk, yogurt, crème fraîche, and fresh cheeses like mozzarella barely budge the needle of the basic umami-meter, owing to the limited enzymatic effect from the brief action of microorganisms. As cheeses get older and more complex—Brie, Gouda, Emmentaler, Cheddar, and such—the umami starts to register. Finally, in long-aged hard cheeses, such as Parmigiano-Reggiano and similar cheeses, the basic umami is practically off the dial. Once again, age is of the umami essence. Blue-veined cheeses like Roquefort and Maytag, though younger than hard cheeses, are similarly umami-rich, an effect they owe to doubly intense enzyme action from both fungus and bacteria.

Fresh goat's milk and sheep's milk are both endowed with more of both kinds of umami, and their cheeses, even when relatively fresh, are more efficient umami delivery vehicles.

Butter is rich and satisfying, but it is not umami.

Eggs, although not dairy, find themselves in the dairy section of markets, and therefore the dairy section of this book. Their umami, considerable when raw (think of the richness of eggnog), is more quickly developed through any form of cooking.

GRAINS

Grains vary widely, but generally seem to be mediocre umami ingredients. Corn is the most striking exception (see Garden Vegetables and Fruits, page 25).

Rice is another—would nigiri sushi taste the same without it? Although the science is sketchy, even contradictory (rice has a decent amount of protein but most appears to be complete, with little free amino acid), surely there is some umami at work here. Or perhaps it is just that rice is one of the foods that benefits most by the addition of umami to the meal. Nonetheless, we count it as umami.

The umami of rice comes to indisputable life when it is fermented, as in rice wine and rice wine vinegars in their many forms, amazake (freshly steamed rice served with fermented rice liquids), and, of course, umami-rich sakes.

Wheat, too, exhibits modest umami until fermented or otherwise processed. Remember that glutamate itself is named for gluten, the protein that gives bread and pasta their strength. That and the very fact that much MSG was once manufactured from wheat is testament to its umami potential. Unfortunately, most mass-manufactured breads, which are induced to rise quickly, never have a chance to develop much umami. But slow-risen artisanal breads, especially those made with sourdough starters and other pre-fermentation techniques (see Umami Poolish Bread recipe, page 44), do the umami trick.

FINFISH, SHELLFISH, AND CEPHALOPODS

Overall, fish tend to be good sources of both basic and synergizing umami.

Among finfish, anchovies, herring, mackerel, sardines, tuna, bluefish, and salmon are the champions, with trout, monkfish, snapper, sea bass, and fish roe (notably caviar) not far behind. All finfish pick up umami when smoked, salt packed, or pickled (for example, gravlax and pickled herring). Even codfish, which is pretty low in umami when fresh, gets a jolt of both basic and synergizing umami when salted and dried, as in baccala and its many variations.

Worthy of special note is katsuobushi, the boiled, dried, smoked, and surface-fermented block of skipjack tuna, suffused with synergizing umami. It is one of the key ingredients in Japanese dashi broth. For a jolt of the umami common in Japanese cuisine, make one of the dashi recipes using katsuobushi: Dr. Ikeda's Soup, page 15, or Nobu's Dashi, page 89.

Shellfish are commendable providers of all umami, including oysters, scallops, mussels, clams, lobsters, sea urchin, shrimp, and crab; so too are squid and octopus.

Because fresh fish are delicate and must be cooked carefully—often briefly, and sometimes not at all—there is not much opportunity to develop additional umami. This is not a problem with most fish, but does indicate the inclusion of sauces, condiments, and other umami ingredients on the plate when serving haddock, sole, and other low-activity fish.

FERMENTED AND PICKLED VEGETABLES AND FRUITS

Fermentation provides an opportunity for the protein and genetic materials in plant foods to break down via enzymatic action without spoiling in the process. Foods are inoculated, either artificially

5. Rinse, rest, and sip, swirl, and swallow the third solution. Note how sour taste is like salt in that it seems sharp and triggers salivation.

6. Rinse, rest, then sip, swirl, and swallow the fourth solution with nostrils closed. Because umami is subtler than other tastes, you might need to mentally seek the savory, meaty sensation in your mouth. By now, you know what tastes taste like, so it should be a little easier.

7. Finally, rinse, rest, and chew the chocolate, making sure to cover the inside of your mouth with it. You won't need to block your nostrils. The bitterness will make itself quite apparent.

CHEAP CHEF TRICK

Poke around the pantries of many good chefs cooking decidedly non-Asian fare, and what do you find? Asian fish sauce—Thai nam pla, Vietnamese nuoc mam and Japanese ishiru, to name a few. It's an old but quiet custom (no one knows how widespread) to spike soups, sauces, dressings, and savory fillings with a scant shot or two of this concentrated umami-in-a-bottle. Not enough to taste fish, for sure, but just enough to bring dull foods to life. Get yourself a bottle and try it. (See Sources, page 194.)

or naturally, with harmless bacteria or fungi that go about digesting parts of the food, producing carbon dioxide and acids, and leaving behind a preserved food with heightened umami, chiefly of the synergizing variety. Salt is often added at the outset to ward off malicious infection until the good-guy microbes get established. Because they are acidic, these foods are often called pickles, but there is also a pickling process that takes place without fermentation.

The nonfermented pickling process involves the immersion of vegetables in a ready-made acid, typically vinegar, which is then heated to kill undesirable microbes that may show up. This also preserves the vegetable, but there is little or no umami creation. If you are seeking umami, look for pickled products that are fermented.

In addition to the famous pickled cucumber, aka kosher dills, fermented plant food products with wonderful character and loads of umami include German sauerkraut, Korean kimchi, olives (black more than green), Hawaiian poi (made from taro and other root vegetables), pickled ginger (a sushi essential), pickled plum (ume), North African pickled lemon, and pickled versions of nearly every vegetable and fruit with a cell structure sufficient to withstand (or get stronger during) the typical pickling ordeal.

It is no accident that we love the umami of fermented foods. The practice encourages survival of our species by seeing to it that we don't waste food, but rather preserve it in times of plenty to enjoy when fresh food is scarce. Meanwhile, fermentation generates amino acids, nucleotides, essential fatty acids, vitamins, antioxidants, and healthy phytosterols, all in forms that are easy for our bodies to assimilate.

When made well, these foods can serve as instant taste-balancing agents, adding salty, sour, umami, and sometimes sweet tastes to dishes in need of verve.

SOY AND SOY PRODUCTS

These deserve a discussion of their own because of the immense contribution the unassuming little soybean makes to umami, especially on the Asian table.

The actual soybean straight from the pod is among the most protein-rich foods on earth, rivaling even meats. And in a feat rare in the vegetable world, it provides complete protein with all nine essential amino acids. Soybeans start out modestly umami, but increase dramatically as they are processed.

Nonfermented soy products include edamame (boiled and salted soybeans served as a snack), soy milk, roasted soy nuts, and tofu (soybean curd). The first two are moderate in umami. Roasted soybeans have a little more, and tofu picks up some more if steamed or stir-fried.

More interesting nutritionally, flavor-wise, and in umami content are the fermented soy products, which include soy sauce (with umami to rival Parmesan cheese), tempeh (fermented soybean curd), natto (soybeans fermented without salt), and miso (long-aged fungus-cultured soy, often mixed with other grains). You will also find a product called fermented bean paste, based on soy mixed with other flavors such as garlic and chili peppers. They all deliver a range of readily available umami amino acids in tangy, tasty preparations.

MUSHROOMS, TRUFFLES, AND OTHER FUNGI

Mushrooms and other fungi are among the finest culinary sources of synergizing umami. They certainly differ in content, but all mushrooms and all truffles (their subterranean cousins) have enough to justify consideration in any recipe that needs an umami lift.

Generally speaking, the deeper the mushrooms' color, the more umami it brings to the table. That rough rule of thumb places shiitakes, portobellos, morels, and porcinis at the top of the umami ranking; oysters, chanterelles, and cremini in the middle; and enoki and white or button mushrooms near the bottom. Dried mushrooms tend to have more umami than fresh.

Truffles turn that rule on its head—with Piedmont's white truffles generally regarded as richer and more intoxicating than the Perigord black.

We must not neglect the most common fungus found in the kitchen—yeast. Not only is yeast a highly regarded umami ingredient in its own right (autolyzed, or self-digested, yeast products are favorite umami ingredients among food chemists), but its enzymatic action helps develop the umami lurking in wheat flour, especially when given time to do its work (see Umami Poolish Bread recipe, page 44).

CONDIMENTS

No discussion of umami is complete without dwelling on fermented fish sauce. As stated in the introduction, the first known consumption of fish sauce dates to the ancient Greeks and Romans, although the practice of making and eating these super-

THE UMAMI–VERSUS–SALT TASTE TEST

This test will help you make two key observations. One is the amplifying effect umami has on salt taste. The other is to "teach" your mouth what salt tastes like so you can then ignore it and get a clearer taste of umami.

Mix ¼ teaspoon of kosher salt into two cups of filtered tap water or nonmineral bottled water, and let it come to room temperature.

Pour one cup of this mixture into another container, into which you mix a match head-size pinch of MSG.

Taste the salt-only mixture and make a mental note of its saltiness. Rinse thoroughly with clear, room-temperature water. Taste this salt-only water again and burn the degree of saltiness into your brain. Rinse again.

Now taste the salt and MSG mixture and note two aspects—first, how the saltiness increases dramatically (far more than the addition of a pinch of MSG could account for), and how there is another brothy, savory taste sensation in your mouth. That sensation is umami.

MASKING BITTER WITH UMAMI

Allow a cup of black coffee to cool to room temperature. Take a small sip, swirl it around in your mouth, and swallow. Concentrate on the bitterness and where in your mouth the sensation is detected. Make a mental note of the intensity of the bitterness (it helps to close your eyes while you taste). Now add a tiny amount (about the size of a pinhead) of Ac'cent or other packaged MSG to the coffee and mix thoroughly. Take another sip, swirl it around, and swallow again. Is the coffee more or less bitter? The bitter-masking properties of umami take the edge off foods with a bitter note.

concentrated umami elixirs probably predates written records. Today, we associate fish sauce with Asian cuisine, and nearly every Asian culture has its own version, some better than others. The types most commonly found in North America are Thai fish sauce, nam pla, and Vietnamese fish sauce, nuoc mam.

Rarer in the West are Japanese ishiru, Philippine patis, Chinese yu-lu, Malaysian budu, Indonesian bakasang, and Myanmarian ngan-pya-ye, each made in a slightly different fashion and producing different results, but all sharing the same basic recipe: Take very fresh fish (usually anchovies or mackerel, but just about every kind of seafood is represented in some fish sauce recipe), mix with salt, set out in the sun to start fermentation, then age in a vat, sometimes for a year or more. When done, draw the sauce off through a spigot, ideally at the bottom of the vat, to reveal a clear, amber-colored liquid with the smell of the ocean and a pleasing fish flavor—not to mention more basic and synergizing umami than any other comestible on Earth. Fish pastes of similar origin are familiar in Asian kitchens, though less available elsewhere.

One enduring Western version of fish sauce is Worcestershire sauce, an intriguingly sweet, salty, tart, and bitter concoction that few devotees realize contains a copious dose of synergizing umami anchovies, skillfully disguised by a number of other assertive ingredients.

But the king of Western umami condiments (when measured in sheer consumption) is surely the indomitable tomato catsup, or ketchup, either way a likely corruption of the Malaysian *keecap* or Chinese *koechiap*, both meaning—you guessed it—fish sauce. Today's versions contain no fish, but they do contain sweet sugar, sour vinegar, salty salt, and red, ripe umami tomatoes—and even a touch of bitter from goodness knows what. No wonder Americans love to slather it on everything. With such a superb balance of aggressive tastes, most folks think catsup makes mediocre food taste good, and good food taste great. Tomato salsas have a related balance of tastes, often with a touch of heat, and are also first-rate sources of umami.

FERMENTED, BREWED, AND DISTILLED BEVERAGES

Sometimes overlooked in umami discussions, no doubt due to the newness of the whole umami discussion itself, are alcoholic beverages, including wine, beer, and spirits.

Wine has received some attention with regard to umami, and while a comprehensive discourse would require a volume by itself, a few guiding principles have emerged. First is that older, earthier, less fruity wines tend to deliver more umami, and pair better with a wider range of foods, particularly those with more complex flavors. For example, a young, tannic, fruit-forward California cabernet sauvignon pairs well with a simply prepared grilled lamb chop, but less so with, say, a subtly flavored braised beef. The California cabernet might taste aggressively coarse and unbalanced with the umami of the dish. On the other hand, a fifteen-year-old French Bordeaux has had the opportunity to create harmonious balance among its tastes, umami included, and actually goes well with either dish.

Logically, then, white wines are unlikely to develop as much umami as reds. And fortified wines like sherry, Madeira, and port, because of their aging and—in the case of those made in the traditions of Jerez, Madeira, and Oporto—ancient provenance, are apt to bring a bounty of umami to the glass.

However, umami does play a leading role in Japan's venerated sake, which is brewed from polished rice. Although there is as much plonk among sakes as there is among grape wines, many better sakes are brewed for and evaluated on their umami content. The best sakes list their amino acids on the label.

The story of umami in beer is a work in process, but with what we know about the enzyme action of yeast on wheat flour, it is an easy leap to believe that hops and grains in beer wort would have a similar response to brewer's yeast. Besides, beer goes great with cheeseburgers, pot roast, pizza, and Asian food, all umami in themselves—proof enough, perhaps, of beer's umaminess.

Among distilled spirits, the leading candidates for umami status are surely the whiskeys and other brown beverages. Again, fermentation and long aging in wooden casks would understandably conspire to create smooth umami effects. It has also been suggested that kokumi (see page 22) is quietly at work, smoothing and enriching these beverages as they age for years on end.

THE ESSENTIAL UMAMI PANTRY

Here are six everyday ingredients we keep on hand for times when a soup needs zip, an entrée needs a lift, or a sauce needs some depth.

1. SOY SAUCE Excellent in marinades, tomato sauces, barbeque sauce, salad dressings, and dipping sauces. A small amount imparts considerable umami, more adds distinctly Asian character. Insist on naturally brewed.

2. WORCESTERSHIRE SAUCE Uses are similar to soy sauce, but the effect is fruitier, and some think it tastes bitter if you use too much. Others like it so much, they keep a bottle at the table.

3. ASIAN FISH SAUCE Use sparingly at first (start with one tablespoon per quart) in all kinds of sauces (even for non-fish dishes), marinades, and dressings. Excellent addition to fish chowders and shell bean and vegetable soups (see Cheap Chef Trick, page 29).

4. CANNED TOMATOES Good quality canned imported tomatoes (whole, crushed, sauce, and paste) will enliven soups, grain and vegetable side dishes, and both veggie- and meat-based main courses.

5. PARMIGIANO-REGGIANO CHEESE Crumble over salads and cooked vegetables, grate over pasta and mashed potatoes, shave to top canapés and other finger foods. Simmer the hard rind in tomato sauces and soups.

6. DRIED SHIITAKE MUSHROOMS Reconstitute in warm water for fifteen minutes (strain and use the soaking liquid in the recipe), chop, and add to sauces and soups, potatoes, grains, pastas, and vegetable sides. Or turn them to shiitake dust in a food processor and sprinkle meats before grilling, pan frying, or roasting, or to garnish side dishes.

EVERYDAY UMAMI RECIPES

For us, cooking with umami is an everyday affair, made simple by the abundance and ubiquity of umami in familiar and easy-to-find ingredients. Following are just a few of our favorite umami recipes for foods you can cook every day. Many of these recipes are umami-charged variations on recipes you may already make. Others you might find a touch more exotic. We hope you find them all easy and delicious.

As clues to one aspect of what makes these recipes work, ingredients contributing significant umami appear in **boldface type**.

COQ AU VIN NOUVEAU

At the risk of committing heresy, we present this quick and easy update to the vener-able Burgundian (and very umami) classic that traditionally calls for bacon, red wine, and a tough old rooster. We have lightened it up with lean smoked ham and your choice of white wine; good matches, we think, for the lighter flavor of thighs from a younger chicken. Make it a day ahead and gently reheat it for even more umami and better developed flavor. Keep a loaf of good French bread nearby, as the gravy is irresistible to sop up.

SERVES 4 FOR DINNER

2	tablespoons extra virgin olive oil
4	ounces lean smoked **ham**, diced medium
8	skinless **chicken thighs**
	Salt and freshly ground black pepper
3	tablespoons all-purpose flour or Wondra
1	medium onion, diced medium
4	cloves garlic, minced
¼	cup minced shallots
1	cup cremini or button **mushroom** slices, ¼-inch thick (⅓ to ½ pound)
1	cup fruity **white wine** such as sauvignon blanc
1	(14-ounce) can low-fat **chicken broth**
2	medium **carrots**, peeled and sliced ½-inch thick
2	stalks celery, sliced ½-inch thick
2	sprigs fresh thyme, or ½ teaspoon dried

1. Choose a heavy Dutch oven or skillet with a tight-fitting cover, large enough to fit the chicken in no more than two layers plus the vegetables. In this pan, heat 1 tablespoon of the oil, add the ham and sauté until browned all over. Remove and reserve the ham, leaving as much of the oil in the pan as you can.

2. Liberally season the pieces of chicken with salt and pepper and dredge them in the flour. Add the remaining oil to pan. When the oil is hot, sear the pieces of chicken thoroughly on all sides until well browned. Take care not to scorch the flour coating, but do let it get brown. Do this in batches. Reserve the chicken with the ham.

3. Return pan to the burner set to medium. Add the onion, garlic, shallots, and mushrooms, and sauté for 3 minutes, stirring constantly, until tender and fragrant. Add the wine, chicken broth, carrots, celery, and thyme, and let the pan come to a boil. Add the reserved chicken and ham. Cover the pot and bring to a simmer. Cook for 45 to 50 minutes, until the chicken is very tender and the sauce has thickened from the flour. Taste and correct seasoning with salt and pepper.

4. Arrange chicken pieces and vegetables on a warmed platter, and cover with the sauce. Serve with rice, noodles, or roasted potatoes.

ASPARAGUS FRITTATA

A frittata is an Italian-style open-faced omelet, cooked slowly on the stovetop and finished under the broiler. Although it is a simple, rustic dish, it takes some time and effort. But it pays off with rich, deep flavors and satisfying textures.

SERVES 2 FOR BRUNCH OR LIGHT LUNCH

6	spears pencil-thin **asparagus**
2	tablespoons olive oil
1	medium red onion, sliced ¼-inch thick
1	small shallot, roughly chopped
½	teaspoon kosher salt
½	cup coarsely grated **Parmigiano-Reggiano cheese**
1	small, ripe Roma **tomato**, diced small
1	tablespoon sliced black **olives** (1 to 2 pitted olives)
¼	teaspoon freshly ground black pepper
4	large **eggs**, lightly beaten

1.   Bring a medium saucepan of salted water to a boil. Wash and trim the asparagus. Cut into ½-inch lengths. Cook in the boiling water until al dente, 1 ½ to 2 minutes. Drain and set aside uncovered.

2.   Heat the olive oil in an 8-inch ovenproof nonstick skillet on a burner set to medium. Add the onions, shallots, and salt, and toss to coat. Caramelize them by cooking them very slowly over low heat (they should barely sizzle), stirring occasionally, until deep golden brown, about 20 minutes. Drain the onions and shallots thoroughly, leaving as much oil in the pan as you can. Set aside to cool.

3.   Thoroughly mix the cheese, tomato, olives, pepper, asparagus, and cooled onions into the beaten eggs. Reheat the oil in the pan over medium heat. When a drop of water tossed into the pan sizzles loudly, add the egg mixture, stirring briefly to distribute the fillings. Turn the burner to low and let the mixture cook slowly. You should see just a few lazy bubbles popping up around the edges. Cook undisturbed until the edges are cooked but the middle is still very liquid, about 8 minutes. While the frittata cooks, preheat the broiler to medium.

4.   Put the pan under the broiler until the top of the frittata is golden brown, the edges are puffed up, and the center is just set (the center will jiggle slightly but pops right back after you poke it), about 2 minutes. Don't overcook it. Loosen with a nonscratch spatula, if needed. Move to a warmed platter and serve right away.

MAXED-OUT MEATLOAF

With apologies to grandmothers everywhere, we humbly suggest that this will become your favorite meatloaf ever. Not because it is radically different—it isn't. But rather, because it's more of what you love meatloaf for: umami. If by some odd chance you don't eat it all for dinner, you'll want to fry up a slice to go with your eggs and toast for breakfast and put a slab between two slices of crusty bread for lunch.

SERVES 6 TO 8 FOR DINNER

2	tablespoons plus 1 teaspoon extra virgin olive oil
2	medium onions, diced medium
2	cloves garlic, minced
5	ounces cremini or other **mushrooms**, sliced ¼-inch thick
1	medium **red bell pepper**
2	**eggs**
2	pounds **ground beef**
1	ripe red **tomato**, diced small then crushed
1	cup **corn** kernels, thawed if frozen, or freshly cooked
1	cup fine dry bread crumbs
3	tablespoons **soy sauce**
2	teaspoons **white truffle oil**
2	teaspoons kosher salt
½	teaspoon freshly ground black pepper
	Olive oil, for brushing
½	pound sliced hickory-smoked **bacon**

1. Preheat the oven to 450 degrees F.

2. Heat 2 tablespoons of the extra virgin olive oil in a large skillet. Add the onions and sauté until translucent, about 4 minutes. Add the garlic and mushrooms, and sauté until the mixture is caramelized, about 6 minutes more. Set aside to cool thoroughly.

3. Core and cut the red bell pepper into quarters. Coat the pepper pieces with the remaining extra virgin olive oil and grill on a stovetop grill or under the broiler until barely cooked through. Cool, chop roughly, and set aside.

4. Beat the eggs in a large bowl. Add the ground beef, cooked vegetables, tomato, corn, bread crumbs, soy sauce, truffle oil, salt, and pepper. Gently mix by hand until just incorporated. Do not overwork the ground beef; if you do, the fat will smear and the meatloaf will be dry and tough.

5. Brush or spray a medium sheet pan with olive oil. Put the meatloaf mixture onto the pan and shape into a loaf twice as wide as it is tall. Drape bacon slices diagonally across the entire loaf, overlapping, to completely cover meat. Secure the ends with several toothpicks.

6. Place in the middle of oven and immediately reduce the heat to 375 degrees F. Bake for 1 hour, or until the internal temperature reaches 155 degrees F. Let rest for 10 minutes before slicing and serving.

SICILIAN TOASTS
(BRUSCHETTA DI SICILIA)

These little canapés are quick, easy, and oh-so-umami satisfying. They are wonderful as an accompaniment to cocktails before dinner, or as a party snack.

MAKES ABOUT 28 CANAPÉS

¼   cup **pine nuts**

7   tablespoons extra virgin olive oil

½   pound eggplant, diced small

1   small onion, diced small

3   cloves garlic, minced

1   medium, ripe red **tomato**, diced small

1   tablespoon freshly squeezed lemon juice, or to taste

     Salt and freshly ground black pepper

1   (15-inch) loaf French bread

1   (3.75-ounce) can **sardines** packed in olive oil

¼   cup shredded fresh basil leaves

½   pound **buffalo mozzarella**

1.   Preheat the oven to 400 degrees F.

2.   Heat a large skillet to medium. Add the pine nuts and toss until golden brown. Reserve.

3.   Return the pan to the burner and turn to high. Add 3 tablespoons of the olive oil to the pan. Add the eggplant and sauté for 3 minutes. Add the onions and sauté for another 2 minutes. Add the garlic and sauté for 1 more minute. Add tomatoes and cook, stirring occasionally, until tomatoes break down. Transfer to a bowl to cool. Add pine nuts and lemon juice and toss. Season well with salt and pepper.

4.   Slice the bread ½-inch thick. Brush both sides of each slice with the remaining olive oil, and sprinkle with salt and pepper. Put the bread slices on a rack over a sheet pan, and bake for 7 to 10 minutes, until toasted.

5.   Meanwhile, put the mozzarella into the freezer for about 15 minutes. This will make it easier to grate. Using the largest holes of a box grater, grate the cheese coarsely.

6.   Drain the sardines. Put about one half a sardine onto each toast. Use a fork to smash it and spread it around. Put some basil onto the sardine, and a generous teaspoon of the vegetable mixture on top of that. Finally, top with some mozzarella.

7.   Put the toasts back on the rack on the sheet pan and bake for 3 to 4 minutes, until the cheese has melted. Serve immediately.

UMAMI POOLISH BREAD

This will remind you of bread from the best artisanal bakers—chewy and flavorful with an earthy and exceptionally satisfying taste. That's the umami, created when the bread proteins and yeast are broken down into basic and synergizing umami during the long pre-fermentation. Poolish is a French baker's term for this technique, also known as a biga in Italian or a sponge in English. Making this can take the better part of a day, but the active time is only about 50 minutes, and results are so worth it.

FOR THE POOLISH PRE-FERMENTATION

2   cups **bread flour**

2   heaping tablespoons vital **wheat gluten**

⅛   teaspoon active dry **yeast** (not quick-rising), taken from the Bread recipe below

2   cups cold spring water

FOR THE BREAD

½   cup warm water (a little warmer than a finger plunged into it), plus additional as needed

4½ teaspoons (or 2 envelopes) active dry **yeast** (not quick-rising)

1   tablespoon sugar

1   cup **bread flour**

2   cups **whole wheat flour** (or 2 additional cups bread flour for white bread)

1   tablespoon kosher salt

    Oil, for preparing the baking pans

    Extra flour, for kneading

TO MAKE THE POOLISH PRE-FERMENTATION: In a large nonreactive bowl, combine the bread flour, vital wheat gluten, yeast, and spring water, and mix thoroughly for 2 minutes. It will look like a loose pancake batter. Cover with plastic wrap and allow to sit in a draft-free area for 12 to 16 hours. In time, it will foam and bubble.

TO MAKE THE BREAD:

1.   In a small nonmetallic bowl or cup, combine the warm water, yeast, and sugar. Mix thoroughly with a fork. After a few minutes, it will foam and bubble.

2.   Combine the poolish pre-fermentation, flours, salt, and yeast mixture in the bowl of a stand mixer fitted with a dough hook. Mix for 1 minute on medium to incorporate. Add splashes of water every 15 seconds until all the flour is fully mixed in and the dough pulls away from the side of the mixer bowl. It should be slightly tacky. Adjust with a little flour or water, as needed. Continue mixing for 8 to 10 minutes or until the dough is smooth and springs back when poked with a finger. Transfer to a greased bowl and cover with plastic wrap and a kitchen towel. Let it rise in a draft-free area for 1 hour, until doubled.

3.   Brush or spray with oil two 9-inch loaf pans. Punch down the dough and transfer to a lightly floured surface. Cut in half with a sharp knife. Shape into cylinders and push into loaf pans. Sprinkle flour generously over the tops and loosely cover with plastic wrap and a kitchen towel. Let rise in a draft-free area for 1 hour or until doubled.

4.   Preheat the oven to 375 degrees F. Bake the bread in the middle of the oven for 50 to 60 minutes, until the tops are golden brown and the loaves sound hollow when tapped. Cool thoroughly before slicing and enjoying.

BAKED EGGS WITH PROSCIUTTO, PEAS, AND MORNAY SAUCE

Here is an excellent way to create an elegant and very umami brunch easily and quickly. Instead of prosciutto, try uncooked small shrimp or diced salmon. You could also use meat or poultry, but cook them before adding.

SERVES 4 FOR BRUNCH OR LUNCH

1   (10 x 10-inch) sheet frozen puff pastry dough (Pepperidge Farm works well)

    Softened unsalted butter or cooking spray, for the pan

4   ounces thinly sliced **prosciutto**, cut into ½-inch strips

2   tablespoons (approximately) frozen baby **peas**, thawed (use blanched, fresh peas, if available)

4   teaspoons unsalted butter, melted

2   teaspoons heavy cream

    Kosher salt and freshly ground black pepper

4   large **eggs**

1   tablespoon cold unsalted butter

1   tablespoon all-purpose flour

1   cup milk

⅓   cup grated **Gruyère cheese**

3   chive spears, snipped into ½-inch pieces

1. Thaw the puff pastry dough according to manufacturer's directions.

2. Set a rack in the top third of the oven and preheat to 400 degrees F.

3. Butter the 4 corner cups of a standard-size 6-cup muffin tin, or apply cooking spray. Place a small amount of water in the 2 empties.

4. Cut the dough into 4 equal squares (5 x 5 inches each), using a sharp knife in a rocking motion through dough.

5. Lay one square centered over a buttered muffin cup. Lift the four points of the pastry dough and hold with one hand while you push the dough firmly into the bottom of the cavity with the other hand. Fold the sides where they overlap and arrange the points into peaks. Repeat with the remaining dough squares in the remaining buttered cavities.

6. Into each puff pastry cavity, place one quarter of the prosciutto, 6 to 8 peas, ½ teaspoon of the melted butter, and ½ teaspoon of the heavy cream. Season with salt and pepper. Crack an egg into small bowl, check for shells, then pour the egg into one puff pastry–lined cavity. Drizzle ½ teaspoon melted butter over egg. Season the egg with salt and pepper. Repeat for the remaining three eggs and puff pastry cavities.

7. Place in the oven on the top rack. Bake until pastry has puffed and turned golden and egg whites are no longer translucent, 25 to 30 minutes.

8. During the last 15 minutes of baking, make the sauce: In small saucepan set over high heat, combine the cold butter and the flour. Whisk together until butter is just melted and flour is blended in. Add the milk and whisk continuously, scraping all surfaces of the pan. Bring to a simmer, adjust heat, and whisk for 1 minute until thick enough to coat a spoon.

9. Take the pan off the heat and add the cheese. Whisk to blend fully. Adjust the seasoning.

10. Set the baked egg pastries on 4 warmed luncheon plates, pour one quarter of the sauce over each, garnish with chives, and serve.

VEGETARIAN MUFFALETTA ROLL-UPS

We slimmed down this signature New Orleans sandwich by reducing the bread from a big, crusty roll to a roll-up, and by turning it vegetarian. But we didn't skimp on the umami. Roasted portobello mushroom is a plausible stand-in for the cold cuts, and the traditional provolone cheese is replaced by lighter, tarter goat cheese for its flavor impact and creamy texture. For best flavor, serve at room temperature.

SERVES 2 FOR LUNCH

6	medium **portobello mushrooms** (about 3 ounces)
	Olive oil, for brushing
½	small **red bell pepper**
¼	cup roughly chopped kalamata **olives**
¼	cup roughly chopped Spanish **olives** with pimentos
3	tablespoons minced celery
1½	teaspoons minced **capers**
2	teaspoons minced fresh parsley
1	small clove garlic, minced
½	teaspoon dried oregano
2	tablespoons extra virgin olive oil
	Salt and freshly ground black pepper
4	ounces soft, fresh **goat cheese,** at room temperature
2	(12-inch) lavash roll-up breads

1.   Preheat the oven to 450 degrees F.

2.   Twist the stems off the portobello mushrooms and scrape the gills out with a teaspoon. Discard stems and gills. Brush or spray the tops with olive oil.

3.   Remove seeds and ribs from the red pepper. Brush or spray with olive oil.

4.   Put the mushroom caps and red pepper on a rack or a sheet pan and roast for 20 minutes, or until the peppers are blistered and the mushrooms begin to toast. Set aside to cool.

5.   In a medium bowl, toss together the olives, celery, capers, parsley, garlic, oregano, and olive oil to combine.

6.   Roughly chop the mushrooms and red pepper and add to the mixture. Add salt and pepper to taste. Allow to sit at room temperature for 10 minutes so the mushrooms plump and the flavors can meld.

7.   Use a spatula to spread half the goat cheese over each lavash. Spread half the filling over the cheese on each. Roll up, slice in half on the bias, and serve.

"RAGUMAMI" TOMATO AND TWO MEAT SAUCE

This sauce is very chunky and exceedingly umami. Serve it with your favorite pasta (spaghetti is a natural), a big tossed salad, and some crusty bread, and you have an easy meal that will delight any crowd. Combining beef and pork gives this an unexpected dimension of meaty flavor. Pecorino Romano is a sharp and tangy sheep's milk cheese that is quite distinctive, but any good quality hard grating cheese will suffice.

SERVES 8 TO 10 FOR DINNER

¼ cup extra virgin olive oil

1 pound **ground beef**

1 pound **ground pork**

1 tablespoon milk

1 cup dry **red wine**

3 small onions, minced

1 medium shallot, minced

1 medium jalapeño pepper, stem and seeds removed, minced

¼ pound **shiitake mushrooms**, diced medium

6 cloves garlic, minced

2 (28-ounce) cans Italian-style **tomatoes**, coarsely chopped

2 tablespoons **Worcestershire sauce**

Salt and freshly ground black pepper

1 tablespoon **red wine vinegar**, or to taste

A generous handful each of fresh basil and cilantro, leaves only

Cooked pasta, for serving

1 cup grated **pecorino Romano cheese**, for sprinkling at the table

1.   Heat 1 tablespoon of the olive oil in a 6-quart saucepan or Dutch oven. Brown the beef and pork in batches (about ½ pound at a time) until well browned, adding a splash of the milk to each batch. Remove and reserve the browned meat. Add ¼ cup of the wine to deglaze the pan, scraping with a wooden spoon to remove any brown bits left behind. Add the wine in the pan to the reserved meat.

2.   Wipe out the pan with a paper towel. Heat the remaining 3 tablespoons olive oil. Sauté the onions and shallots until translucent. Add the jalapeño pepper, mushrooms, and garlic, and sauté 2 minutes more, taking care not to burn the garlic. Add the remaining wine, stir and scrape with a wooden spoon. Boil the mixture for 2 minutes or until the wine is almost gone. Add the browned meat, the tomatoes, 2¾ cups water, and the Worcestershire sauce. Simmer for 1 hour or until it reaches the desired texture, stirring occasionally. Add salt, pepper, and red wine vinegar to taste. Turn off the heat and add the basil and cilantro leaves, stirring them in until they wilt. Serve over your choice of pasta, and sprinkle with the pecorino.

LAMB TAGINE

This dish is inspired by the tagine cooking tradition of North African cuisine, fragrantly accented with spices and slow-cooked in the embers of a fire in the characteristic funnel-shaped vessel. A Dutch oven or heavy pot, placed on a modern stovetop, makes a suitable substitute. The harmonious melding of sweet and savory, along with the scent of toasted spices weaving through the flavor layers, presents a grand and delightfully balanced umami experience. You will find each bite lingers on the palate, even as your fork returns to your plate for more.

SERVES 6 TO 8 FOR DINNER

2   tablespoons olive oil

1   boneless **leg of lamb** (about 3½ to 4 pounds), tied or netted
     Salt and freshly ground black pepper

2   medium onions, sliced ½-inch thick

1½ teaspoons ground coriander

1½ teaspoons ground cumin

1½ teaspoons ground cinnamon

6   whole cloves

6   cloves garlic, sliced thin

1   tablespoon minced fresh ginger

1   (14-ounce) can **beef broth**

1   (14-ounce) can **chicken broth**

3   medium **carrots**, peeled and sliced ½-inch thick

½   cup raisins

½   cup dried apricots, quartered

½   cup kalamata **olives**, pitted and roughly chopped

2   tablespoons honey

2   tablespoons roughly chopped cilantro
     Grated zest and juice of ½ lemon
     Cooked couscous or **rice**, for serving

1. Heat 1 tablespoon of the olive oil in a heavy 4-quart pot over high heat. Liberally season the leg of lamb with salt and pepper. When the oil begins to smoke, sear lamb thoroughly on all sides until well browned. Remove from pan and reserve.

2. Lower heat to medium-high. Add the remaining olive oil and the onions. Sauté, stirring occasionally, until golden brown, about 10 minutes. Add the coriander, cumin, cinnamon, cloves, garlic, and ginger, and sauté while stirring and scraping with a wooden spoon, until very fragrant, about 2 minutes. Add the beef and chicken broth and boil vigorously for 10 minutes with cover off.

3. Return the lamb to the pot. The liquid should cover the lamb by one half to two thirds. Add water, or remove and reserve cooking liquid, as needed. Cover the pot and adjust the heat to a simmer. After 1½ hours, turn the lamb over and add the carrots, raisins, apricots, olives, and honey, and stir in. Cover and return to a simmer.

4. Cook 30 minutes to 1 hour more, until the lamb is very tender and separates easily with a fork. Remove the lamb from the pot and keep warm. Skim excess fat from the sauce. (If you removed cooking liquid earlier, add it to the sauce now.) Boil the sauce 5 minutes to reduce. Adjust the seasoning with salt and pepper, and finish with the cilantro and lemon juice and zest.

5. Cut the strings away from the lamb. Unfold the roast and remove the veins of fat, if desired, and refold. Carve lamb across the grain into ½-inch slices. Place the slices on warm platter atop couscous or rice, ladle with sauce, and serve.

THE CHEFS AND THEIR UMAMI RECIPES

We were delighted, and to some degree even surprised, by the enthusiasm and generous support of so many gifted chefs when invited to participate in this book project. Umami has surely taken hold in American restaurant kitchens and the work of these chefs is delicious proof.

You will see a very wide range of recipes and cooking styles represented in these pages—some simple, others complex; some using everyday ingredients, others relying on the exotic. It is our hope that these recipes will give you insight, not only into the culinary cogitations of these masterful chefs, but also into the limitless ways umami can and is being used in America today. And with that, we hope you find inspiration for your own umami creations.

Throughout these recipes, ingredients contributing significant umami appear in **boldface type**.

BRAISED DUCK LEGS WITH MUSHROOMS AND CAPER-VINEGAR SAUCE

JODY ADAMS

Jody confesses that umami is as new to her as it is to most American chefs, yet a glance down this list of ingredients belies that claim. Like so many other great chefs, she cooks from a keenly developed sense of what tastes good, and more often than not, that sense leads her to umami.

This dish is all about the deep flavors and richly layered umami that Jody creates with a variety of basic and synergizing umami ingredients. These include a medley of mushrooms, each with a different flavor note, plus tomato, sherry, chicken stock, and capers. Slow cooking ensures maximum umami development in the duck and a sauce that marries sweet, sour, salty, and savory more deeply each minute it cooks.

SERVES 4

- ¼ cup kosher salt
- 2 tablespoons plus 1 teaspoon coarsely chopped fresh thyme
- 4 **duck leg** quarters
- ½ ounce dried **porcini mushrooms**
  Freshly ground black pepper
- ¾ pound assorted fresh **mushrooms,** wiped clean, stem ends removed, and cut into bite-size pieces if large
- 2 shallots, sliced thin
- 2 leeks (white and light green parts only), sliced ¼-inch thick, washed, and drained
- 4 garlic cloves, smashed
- 4½ teaspoons **tomato** paste
- 1 cup dry **sherry**
- 2 cups **chicken stock**
- 2 tablespoons **sherry vinegar**
- 1 tablespoon rinsed **capers**
- 4 sprigs thyme, for garnish

1.   Combine the kosher salt and 2 tablespoons of the thyme in a blender. Process until the thyme is finely chopped and the salt is bright green. Push the salt mixture through a fine sieve into a bowl. Season the duck legs all over with half of the thyme-salt. Set on a rack in a pan and refrigerate, uncovered, overnight.

2.   Soak the porcini mushrooms in ½ cup warm water at least 30 minutes, until reconstituted. Remove the mushrooms and carefully strain the soaking liquid to remove any grit or sand; reserve. Clean and coarsely chop the mushrooms, and reserve.

3.   While the mushrooms are soaking, using a paper towel, rub the duck legs to remove excess salt and moisture. Season the duck legs with pepper. Heat a large sauté pan over medium heat. Add the legs, skin side down, reduce the heat to medium-low, and cook for 10 minutes, until the fat has started to render and the skin is crisp. Transfer the legs to a plate. Pour all but 1 tablespoon of the rendered fat into a heatproof container and reserve.

4.   Increase the heat to medium-high. Cook the fresh mushrooms in 2 batches until tender, adding duck fat if necessary. Add the shallots and cook, tossing frequently, until tender, about 3 minutes. Season with some of the remaining thyme-salt and pepper. Transfer to a plate and reserve.

5.   Add 1 tablespoon duck fat to the pan. Add the leeks and garlic and season with thyme-salt and pepper, and cook until tender and golden brown, about 8 minutes. Add the tomato paste and cook for 3 minutes. Add the reconstituted porcini mushrooms, the soaking liquid, and the sherry. Reduce the heat to medium, and cook until the liquid has reduced to about ¼ cup. Add the chicken stock and reduce by one third.

6.   Add the duck legs. The liquid should come halfway up the side of the legs. If there is too much liquid, remove the duck legs, increase the heat to reduce the liquid further, and put the duck legs back in. Cover with parchment paper cut to the diameter of the pan, and then a lid. Reduce the heat to low and cook the legs very slowly for 1½ hours. Add the mushrooms, cover, and cook an additional 30 minutes, or until the duck legs are very tender.

7.   Preheat the broiler. Transfer the legs to a baking sheet, skin side up, and pat dry.

8.   Strain the cooking juices into a glass container and put in the freezer for 10 minutes. Skim the fat off the top and discard. Put the juices back in the pan with the mushrooms. Add the vinegar and capers and bring to a boil. Add the remaining 1 teaspoon of chopped thyme. Keep warm.

9.   Position the duck legs under the broiler until the skin is crisp. To serve, put a duck leg on a plate, add a spoonful of mushrooms and sauce. Garnish with thyme sprigs and serve.

CORN AND CHIVE PANNA COTTA WITH TOMATO SALAD AND PARMESAN FRICO

JODY ADAMS

This recipe, like all of Jody's, starts with seasonal ingredients. In this case, it is fresh corn on the cob and vine-ripe tomatoes, both rich in basic umami. Next, she layers on synergizing umami with the Parmesan frico and anchovies in the dressing. The sweet and creamy panna cotta, crunchy Parmesan frico, and sweet, sour, and savory flavors of the dressing are an excellent example of maximized fifth-taste effect. And the combination serves as a case in point of what can be achieved with simple ingredients and sound balance among tastes, flavors, and textures.

There are a number of steps to this recipe, but each one is easy and well worth the effort.

SERVES 4 AS AN APPETIZER

FOR THE PANNA COTTA

1   tablespoon vegetable oil

2   large ears freshly picked sweet **corn**

3½ cups plus 2 tablespoons whole milk

     Kosher salt and freshly ground white pepper

1   envelope (1 tablespoon) unflavored powdered gelatin

½   cup **crème fraîche**

4½ teaspoons chopped chives

FOR THE PARMESAN FRICO

¼   cup finely ground **cornmeal**

1   cup freshly grated **Parmesan cheese**

FOR THE TOMATO SALAD

½   teaspoon minced shallots

¼   teaspoon minced garlic

2   whole **anchovies** or 4 fillets, cleaned, rinsed, and minced

½   teaspoon Dijon mustard

1   tablespoon **red wine vinegar**

¼   cup extra virgin olive oil

½   pint ripe red Sweet 100 **tomatoes** (or any small, ripe,
       red tomato such as cherry or grape tomatoes), cut in half

½   cup flat-leaf parsley leaves

TO MAKE THE PANNA COTTA:

1.   Brush four 6-ounce custard cups with a thin coating of vegetable oil.

2.   Cut the corn kernels from the cobs with a sharp knife. Scrape off the corn milk with the back of the knife and reserve. Chop each cob into 4 pieces.

3.   Combine the cobs with 3½ cups milk in a small saucepan and cook over medium heat for 15 minutes to extract more flavor. Remove the cobs, capturing as much liquid as possible by scraping with a spoon, and discard.

4.   Add the kernels to the milk, season with salt and pepper, bring to a boil and cook 3 minutes. Cool 5 minutes.

5.   Puree the mixture in a blender or food processor until smooth. Strain through a fine-mesh strainer, pushing with the back of a spoon to extract the liquid. Discard the corn skins.

6.   Sprinkle the gelatin over the remaining 2 tablespoons cold milk. When translucent, whisk the mixture into the warm corn milk for 1 minute, until the gelatin has dissolved. Cool to room temperature.

7.   Whisk in the crème fraîche and chives. Taste and adjust seasonings if necessary. Pour into the prepared custard cups. Chill in the refrigerator until set, about 4 hours.

TO MAKE THE PARMESAN FRICO: Preheat the oven to 375 degrees F. Mix the cornmeal thoroughly with the cheese and sprinkle evenly in a thin layer over a nonstick baking mat on a cookie sheet. Bake until lacy and crisp, 8 to 10 minutes. Allow to cool and break into large shards. Reserve in an airtight container.

TO MAKE THE SALAD: In a small bowl, mix the shallots, garlic, anchovies, mustard, and vinegar together. Whisking constantly, add the oil in a slow steady stream. The dressing will thicken into an emulsion. You can also do this in a blender at the slowest speed. Toss the tomatoes in a bowl with the parsley leaves and dressing. Season with salt and pepper.

TO SERVE: Run a hot knife around the panna cotta in each custard cup and turn it out by inverting it onto a plate. Arrange the tomato salad around the panna cotta and garnish with frico shards.

SPICY CHIPOTLE PORK TACOS WITH SUN-DRIED TOMATO SALSA
(TACOS DE PUERCO ENCHIPOTLADO CON SALSA DE JITOMATE PASADO)

RICK BAYLESS

Rick Bayless has declared it his mission to study, preserve, and share the rich and glorious recipes of authentic Mexican cuisine. Not surprisingly, much of its richness and glory comes from its generous inclusion of basic umami ingredients, especially items such as corn and tomatoes, indigenous to the region (the same holds for beans, which make an outstanding accompaniment to these tacos). Pork and olives provide synergizing umami. The dish is balanced by a touch of tartness from the orange juice and lime, and a smoky note of spice and heat from the chipotle en adobo.

SERVES 4 AS A LIGHT MEAL

2	**pork tenderloins** (about 1 pound total)
1	(7-ounce) can chipotle chilis en adobo
1	cup freshly squeezed orange juice
1	cup **sun-dried tomatoes**, halved (about 2 ounces)
1	small red onion, finely chopped (a generous ½ cup)
½	cup chopped, pitted kalamata **olives**
½	cup chopped fresh cilantro
	About 1 tablespoon freshly squeezed lime juice
	Salt
1	tablespoon rich-tasting lard, vegetable oil, or bacon drippings
12	fresh **corn tortillas**

1.   Lay each tenderloin on a cutting board and cut it in half crosswise. For each piece, make a horizontal cut—you'll be cutting parallel with the board—from one long side to within ¼-inch of the other. This will allow you to fold open the meat like a book, using the uncut side as a hinge. Pound the pork with a meat pounder or heavy mallet to between ½- and ¼-inch thick.

2.   In a food processor or blender, thoroughly puree the chipotles and all the canning sauce. With a brush, liberally paint each piece of meat on both sides with the pureed chipotles. Cover and refrigerate for at least 1 hour but no more than 24 hours or the chipotles will overpower the pork flavor. (There will be considerably more chipotle puree than you need; cover and refrigerate the leftover for up to 2 weeks and use it to marinate other meat, fish, poultry, or vegetables.)

3.   In a small nonreactive saucepan bring the orange juice just to a boil. Add the sun-dried tomatoes, stir well, cover, and remove from the heat. Let stand, stirring once or twice, until softened, about 20 minutes.

4.   Scrape the soaked tomatoes and orange juice into a food processor or blender, and add 1 tablespoon of chipotle puree. Pulse until the tomatoes are rather finely chopped (not pureed). Scrape into a small serving bowl.

5.   Rinse the chopped onion under cold water, shake off the excess liquid and add it to the tomatoes along with the olives, cilantro, and lime juice. Stir, taste, and season with about ¼ teaspoon salt. Adjust the consistency to that of an easily spoonable salsa with additional lime juice or water if necessary. Set aside at room temperature while you cook the meat.

6.   Set a large (12-inch), well-seasoned cast-iron skillet or griddle over medium-high heat. Add the lard, brushing or spreading it around to evenly coat the surface. When the oil just begins to smoke, lay on one of the marinated meat pieces. Sear on one side 2 to 3 minutes, flip it over, and sear the other side about 90 seconds. Transfer to a baking sheet and keep warm in the oven. Sear the remaining meat and set on the baking sheet in a single layer.

7.   To heat the tortillas, fill a vegetable steamer with ½ inch water. Bring to a boil. Wrap the tortillas in a kitchen towel and lay in the steamer. Cover and boil for one minute; turn the heat off and let stand covered for 15 minutes.

8.   Meanwhile, chop or slice the meat into smallish pieces and scoop into a warm serving bowl. Serve with the salsa and warm tortillas.

WHOLE FISH BRAISED WITH TOMATOES, CAPERS, OLIVES, AND HERBS
(PESCADO À LA VERACRUZANA)

RICK BAYLESS

For all its drama on the table, this is a rather straightforward preparation using commonplace ingredients and techniques. Bayless achieves basic and synergized umami with a simple and very successful combination of fish, tomatoes, olives, and capers, nicely balanced with garlic, spices, and chilis. The most important point to remember in preparing this dish is to not be intimidated by cooking a whole fish. There are no special tricks to it, and fish tastes better cooked on the bone.

If you can't obtain snapper, you can use grouper, striped bass, black bass, or pompano—any firm, meaty whole fish. Ask the fishmonger to clean and scale it, cut out the red gills, and trim off the fins at the top, bottom, and alongside the gills.

The sauce keeps well for a day or two in the refrigerator, if you want to make it ahead.

SERVES 4 TO 6

1	whole **snapper** (about 4 pounds)
	Juice of 2 limes
	Salt
3	pounds ripe round **tomatoes** (6 medium-large)
¼	cup olive oil, preferably extra virgin
1	medium white onion, thinly sliced
4	large cloves garlic, finely chopped
3 or 4	bay leaves
1½	teaspoons dried oregano, preferably Mexican
3	tablespoons roughly chopped flat-leaf parsley leaves
1	cup sliced pitted green **olives**, preferably Manzanilla
¼	cup **capers**, drained and rinsed

3   pickled jalapeño peppers, stemmed, seeded, and thinly sliced,
     or 6 whole pickled long guero chilis
     Flat-leaf parsley sprigs, for garnish

1. Cut two parallel diagonal slashes across each side of the fish, starting the first one near the top of the head and angling down toward the tail; cut down through the flesh to the backbone. Put the fish into a large baking dish. Drizzle both sides with the lime juice and sprinkle liberally with salt, about ½ tablespoon per side. Cover and refrigerate for about 1 hour (but no more than 4 hours).

2. Peel the tomatoes, if you like. Core and dice into ½-inch pieces. You should have about 7 cups. Reserve.

3. In a 4- or 5-quart Dutch oven or Mexican cazuela, heat the oil over medium heat. Add the onion and cook, stirring regularly, until just beginning to brown, about 5 minutes. Add the garlic and cook 1 minute more, stirring several times. Raise the heat to medium-high and add the tomatoes, bay leaves, oregano, parsley, half of the olives, half of the capers, and half of the chilis. Simmer briskly, stirring frequently, for about 5 minutes to evaporate some of the liquid. Reduce the heat to medium-low, stir in 1 cup of water and simmer for 15 minutes. Taste and season with salt, about 1 teaspoon. If not using directly, refrigerate in a covered container.

4. Preheat the oven to 350 degrees F. Lightly oil a roasting pan large enough to hold the fish comfortably. Remove the fish from the lime mixture and lay the fish in the pan. (If the tail sticks out of the pan, crimp a piece of oiled aluminum foil around it to prevent burning.) If you made the sauce ahead, reheat it. Cover the fish with the steaming tomato sauce. Bake in the center of the oven 50 to 55 minutes, until the flesh flakes when firmly yet gently pressed where the body meets the head, just above the gills (this is the thickest part).

5. Using 2 sturdy metal spatulas, carefully transfer the fish to a large serving platter. Tip up the roasting pan to collect the sauce and spoon it over the fish. Sprinkle with the remaining olives, capers, and chilis and decorate with sprigs of parsley.

NOTE. To carve the fish, first scrape the tomato sauce away. Use a sharp knife (a boning or filleting knife works best) to begin cutting where the head meets the body, along the top of the fish down to the gill area, going all the way down to the bone. At the gill area, turn the knife horizontally and cut straight down the length of the fish to the tail. Turn the fish so that you're facing its top. Now, still holding your knife horizontally, slice into the meat just above the backbone, starting where the head meets the flesh and continuing all the way to the tail. Keep cutting farther until you free the fillet. Cut the fillet into 3 pieces using the slashes you made before cooking, then use a spatula to transfer the pieces to plates, spooning sauce generously over each. Lift off the now-exposed skeleton, starting at the tail and holding down the bottom fillet with the spatula. Now repeat with the second fillet.

SHORT RIBS BRAISED IN RED WINE WITH CELERY DUO

DANIEL BOULUD

This is one of Daniel Boulud's signature dishes, abounding with sophisticated flavors and deeply developed aromas, and with a delightful lingering finish following every bite. It is also a superb illustration of how well rooted umami is even in classical French cuisine, to which this recipe owes its heritage. The ribs, tomato paste, potatoes, and broth all contribute to the umami, both basic and synergizing, but an enormous part of the umami punch comes from the extended reduction of a generous amount of wine. For best results, use good wine.

The chef recommends browning the short ribs very well at the beginning (à la kokumi) in order to develop the best flavors for the sauce.

SERVES 8

3   (750 ml) bottles dry **red wine**

2   tablespoons vegetable oil

8   **beef short ribs** (about 4 to 4½ pounds), trimmed of excess fat
     Salt and crushed black peppercorns
     Flour, for dredging

8   large shallots, peeled and cut in half

2   medium **carrots**, peeled and sliced 1-inch thick

2   stalks celery, peeled and sliced 1-inch thick

1   medium leek (white and light green parts only),
     coarsely chopped, washed and drained

10 cloves garlic

6 sprigs flat-leaf parsley

2 bay leaves

2 sprigs thyme

2 tablespoons **tomato paste**

3 quarts unsalted **beef broth**

Freshly ground white pepper

Celery Root Puree, for serving (page 66)

Braised Celery, for serving (page 67)

1. Pour the wine into a large saucepan set over medium heat. When the wine is hot, carefully set it aflame. Let the flames die out, then increase the heat so the wine boils; allow it to cook down by half. Remove from the heat.

2. Center a rack in the oven and preheat to 350 degrees F.

3. Warm the oil in a large, heavy, ovenproof pot over medium-high heat. Season the ribs all over with salt and the crushed pepper. Dust half of the ribs with about 1 tablespoon flour. When the oil is hot, slip the ribs into the pot and sear 4 to 5 minutes on each side, until well browned. Transfer to a plate. Repeat with remaining ribs. Remove all but 1 tablespoon of the fat from the pot, lower the heat to medium, and add the shallots, carrots, celery, leek, garlic, parsley, bay leaves, and thyme. Brown the vegetables lightly, 5 to 7 minutes. Stir in the tomato paste and cook for 1 minute.

4. Add the reduced wine, ribs, and stock to the pot. Bring to a boil, cover tightly, and place in the oven to braise for 2½ hours or until the ribs are very tender. Every 30 minutes, skim and discard the fat from the surface. (It's best to make the recipe to this point, cool, and chill the ribs, vegetables, and juices in the pot overnight. Scrape off the fat the next day and reheat before continuing.)

5. Carefully transfer the meat to a platter; keep warm. Boil the pan liquid until it has reduced to 1 quart. Season with salt and white pepper and pass through a fine strainer; discard the solids. (The ribs and sauce can be combined and kept covered in the refrigerator for 2 to 3 days. Reheat gently, basting frequently, on top of the stove or in a 350-degree F oven.)

6. To serve, spoon the Celery Root Puree into the center of 8 plates and top each with a short rib. Lay one piece of Braised Celery over each serving. Pour the sauce onto the plate around the puree.

CELERY ROOT PUREE

4   cups whole milk

2   tablespoons coarse sea salt

2   pounds celery root, peeled and cut into 8 pieces

1   pound Yukon Gold **potatoes**, peeled and cut in half

6   tablespoons (¾ stick) unsalted butter, softened

     Salt and freshly ground white pepper

1. Place the milk, salt, celery root, potatoes, and 4 cups water in a large saucepan; bring to a boil. Lower the heat; simmer until the vegetables are very tender, 20 to 25 minutes; drain and return them to the pan.

2. Place the pan over low heat to cook off excess moisture. Transfer the vegetables to a food processor. Add the butter and puree until just smooth and creamy. Season with salt and pepper. Keep warm.

BRAISED CELERY

2 bunches celery

1 tablespoon extra virgin olive oil

1 **carrot**, peeled and quartered

1 turnip, peeled and quartered

Salt and freshly ground white pepper

2½ cups unsalted **chicken stock**

1. Trim the bottom of each celery bunch (make sure the ribs remain together); then measure 5 inches up from the bottom and cut off the celery tops at that point (you'll be using the bottom end). Remove and discard the 3 or 4 tough outer ribs. Remove any stringy parts with a vegetable peeler; cut each bunch of celery lengthwise into quarters.

2. Warm the oil in a large sauté pan or skillet over medium heat. Add the carrot, turnip, and celery quarters; season with salt and pepper and cook 3 minutes. Pour in the stock and bring to a boil.

3. Adjust the heat so that the stock simmers steadily. Cook the vegetables for about 25 minutes, until they are very tender and the liquid is nearly gone. You should have tender vegetables lightly glazed with the broth. Remove and discard the carrots and turnips. Serve the celery immediately.

SEA SCALLOPS WITH MASHED POTATOES AND RED ONION CONFIT

D A N I E L   B O U L U D

This simple but satisfying dish from Daniel is easy to make, easy to serve, and truly easy to enjoy.

The main ingredients, scallops and potatoes, deliver synergizing and basic umami respectively, backed up by the balsamic vinegar (use the best you can afford) and chicken stock. Daniel achieves balance with sweetness from the scallops, mashed potatoes, and red onion confit; tartness from the vinegar; and salt from careful seasoning. There is a seemingly small but powerfully appealing range of soft, luxurious textures from the potatoes, scallops, and onions that is both comforting and pleasurable.

SERVES 4

1   pound baking **potatoes**, peeled and cut into 1-inch dice
    Salt
4   tablespoons (½ stick) unsalted butter, at room temperature
½   cup heavy cream, warmed
    Freshly ground black pepper
    Pinch of freshly grated nutmeg
2   cups ⅛-inch-thick slices red onions
       (approximately 2 large onions)
3   tablespoons aged **balsamic vinegar**
16 jumbo sea **scallops** (about 1½ pounds), cleaned and patted dry
¼   cup Wondra or all-purpose flour
¼   cup **chicken stock**
    Leaves of 4 sprigs flat-leaf parsley, coarsely chopped

1. Combine the potatoes with 2 quarts water and 2 teaspoons salt in a large sauce-pan over high heat. Bring to a boil and boil until tender, about 20 minutes. Drain and mash the potatoes through a sieve or food mill into the top of a double boiler. Add 2 tablespoons of the butter and the warm heavy cream and stir until smooth. Season with salt, pepper, and nutmeg. To keep the mashed potatoes warm until ready to serve, place the double boiler (with hot water in the bottom pot) over very low heat. Cover with plastic wrap to prevent drying.

2. Melt 1 tablespoon of the butter in a large skillet over medium-low heat. Add the onions, season with salt and pepper, and sweat until very soft. Add 2 tablespoons of the balsamic vinegar. Cook until the onions start to caramelize, about 10 to 15 minutes. When brown, remove from the heat and set aside.

3. Preheat a large nonstick skillet over medium heat. Salt and pepper each scallop and dredge with flour, shaking off any excess. Add ½ tablespoon of the butter to the hot pan. Add the scallops and sauté them for 2 minutes on each side. Sprinkle on the remaining tablespoon of vinegar, add the chicken stock, toss well, and cook for 2 minutes. Remove the scallops from the pan, reduce the sauce by half, and stir in the remaining ½ tablespoon of the butter. Test for seasoning and sprinkle with half of the chopped parsley.

4. To serve, spread the onions on the bottom of 4 warmed shallow plates or a serving platter. Spoon mashed potatoes over the onions and place the scallops on top. Spoon the sauce over the scallops. Sprinkle with the rest of the chopped parsley.

ASPARAGUS SALAD WITH ROASTED PEPPERS AND SHAVED PARMIGIANO-REGGIANO

GARY DANKO

Unlike some American chefs who are just learning about the culinary clout of umami, Gary Danko has been a disciple for many years. His menu of spirited, seasonal dishes, like this lively Asparagus Salad, shows it.

In this, Gary has combined basic umami powerhouse asparagus with synergizing capers, olives, and Parmigiano–Reggiano for an ample umami effect. But just as important, Gary knows that umami by itself is an incomplete experience, so he has layered in a range of tastes including sweet (from roasted red peppers), sour (from tarragon vinegar), salty (from capers, olives, and Parmesan) and pungent (from mustard, garlic, and onions), and complemented them with an equally wide range of textures and aromas.

It looks innocent enough, but this is a powerfully satisfying eating experience.

SERVES 6

1½ to 2 pounds pencil or medium green **asparagus**, trimmed

2 thick-walled **red bell peppers**

Vegetable oil, for brushing

2 tablespoons tarragon vinegar

4 tablespoons minced red onion

1 clove garlic, minced

2 tablespoons **capers**, drained

¼ teaspoon kosher salt

¼ teaspoon freshly ground black pepper

1 tablespoon Dijon mustard

2 teaspoons chopped tarragon or dill

6 tablespoons extra virgin olive oil

6 tablespoons freshly grated **Parmigiano-Reggiano**

4 ounces **goat cheese**, crumbled (optional)

12 niçoise or oil-cured **olives**

1. Bring a large pot of lightly salted water to the boil. Prepare an ice bath by combining equal parts water and ice in a large bowl.

2. Cook the asparagus in the rapidly boiling water for 2 to 4 minutes, until tender. Plunge asparagus into ice bath and cool completely. Drain well and keep chilled until needed.

3. Preheat oven to 375 degrees F. Brush the peppers with vegetable oil. Place on a sheet pan and roast for 30 to 40 minutes, until peppers blister. Remove from oven and place in a bowl. Cover with plastic wrap or a cover, and let rest for 30 minutes. Peel under running water. Cut the peppers open, remove ribs and seeds. Cut into ¼-inch strips.

4. Combine the vinegar, onion, garlic, capers, salt, pepper, mustard, and tarragon in a bowl. Whisk in the oil.

5. Arrange the asparagus on plate, arrange peppers at base of asparagus. Drizzle dressing over asparagus. Sprinkle with Parmigiano-Reggiano and goat cheese (if using). Garnish with olives and serve.

THAI DUCK AND COCONUT SOUP

GARY DANKO

In Thailand, nam pla (Thai fermented fish sauce) is used in an astonishing number of dishes, even in those where some might guess it doesn't belong. Here, for example, we find it in an amount just below the point where it is discernable, in a soup with duck as the principal ingredient. Considering the other basic and synergizing umami ingredients, this would be quite delicious without the nam pla. But with it, this soup is truly memorable.

Although some people might choose to substitute chicken stock for the duck stock, it is not the same. Make your own duck stock by simply using duck instead of chicken in any good chicken stock recipe, or use store-bought duck stock. Duck stock is noticeably richer with a distinct quality.

Kaffir lime leaves and lemongrass are essential to the Thai character of this dish. Together, they create a brisk, refreshing flavor. Both are available online, from Asian grocers (see Sources, page 194), and increasingly in gourmet shops.

Be sure to stir in the last ingredients just before you are ready to serve this soup so they have optimal texture and retain their distinct flavors.

SERVES 6

2	cups **duck stock**
2	stalks lemongrass, white inner core only, minced
2	kaffir lime leaves
1	small fresh chili, seeds removed, minced
4	cups coconut milk
4	tablespoons freshly squeezed lime juice
4	tablespoons **nam pla fish sauce**
	Salt
2	ounces **shiitake mushroom caps**, sliced ¼-inch thick
2	scallions, sliced very thin on the diagonal
½	pound firm **tofu**, cut into small cubes
	Meat from 1 smoked **duck breast**, sliced thin

In a large saucepan, combine the duck stock, lemongrass, lime leaves, and chili, and simmer for 1 hour uncovered. Add the coconut milk and lime juice, nam pla, and salt to taste. Bring to a boil. Stir in mushrooms, scallions, tofu, and duck. Serve immediately.

WILD MUSHROOMS IN A POTATO SHELL ACCENTED WITH CARAMELIZED VEGETABLE JUS

HUBERT KELLER

Hubert Keller shows us how to pack meaty punch into meatless fare by maximizing umami—first with basic umami from umami vegetables, then synergizing umami from an assortment of fresh and dried mushrooms. A touch of soy sauce and sherry vinegar rounds it out.

Hubert calls his creation "a vibrant, healthful, and delicious vegetarian dish, full of explosive flavors. When you serve it, do not forget to pass the pepper mill: wild mushrooms and freshly ground pepper are two great complementary flavors."

Because moisture varies considerably in mushrooms, you may find you need a bit more liquid than the one cup of water called for. If needed, add a little more until you achieve the consistency of a very thick stew.

SERVES 4

- 1 ounce dried **porcinis** or **black chanterelle mushrooms**, or a combination of both
- 10 stemmed **shiitake**, **morel**, or **golden chanterelle mushrooms**, or a combination
- 2 tablespoons minced shallots
- 3 tablespoons olive oil
  Salt and freshly ground black pepper
- 1 small onion, sliced thin
- 1 small **carrot**, peeled and sliced thin
- 1 small leek, white part only, julienned 1-inch long by ⅛-inch thick, washed and drained

2   tablespoons **sherry vinegar**

8   basil leaves, chopped roughly

2   tablespoons minced parsley

1   teaspoon minced garlic

1   tablespoon **soy sauce**

2   tablespoons finely sliced chives

1   medium **tomato,** peeled, seeded, and diced ¼-inch

4   medium Idaho **potatoes** washed, skin on

4   sprigs thyme

1. Combine the porcini mushrooms and 1 cup warm water and soak for at least 30 minutes. Remove the mushrooms. Carefully strain the soaking liquid to remove any grit or sand, and reserve.

2. Dice the porcinis and the fresh mushrooms. In a nonstick sauté pan over medium heat, sauté the mushrooms and shallots in 2 tablespoons of the oil until the shallots just begin to color. Season to taste and reserve. Heat the remaining 1 tablespoon oil in a saucepan. Add the onions, carrot, and leek, and sauté them until golden brown. Deglaze with the sherry vinegar, scraping the bottom of the pan with a wooden spoon to remove any brown bits that remain. Add the soaking liquid from the porcinis, the basil, parsley, garlic, soy sauce, salt, and pepper. Bring to a boil and simmer for 12 to 15 minutes. Let cool slightly, then puree the liquid and vegetables in a blender until smooth.

3. Strain through a fine-mesh sieve into a small saucepan; add the cooked mushrooms, chives, and tomato, and bring to a boil. Remove from heat. Check seasoning and keep covered while preparing the potato shells.

4. Cut a ½-inch-thick slice off both ends of each potato so they stand up straight. Scoop out the insides with a melon baller, taking care not to break through the skin or the bottom. Bring 2 quarts of salted water to a boil. Add the potatoes, lower the heat, and simmer gently 8 to 10 minutes, until potatoes are tender. Carefully remove them from the water and drain well.

5. Transfer the potato shells to a serving platter and set them upright on one cut end, scooped end up. Fill each potato with the mushroom ragout. Spoon the remaining mushroom ragout around. Garnish with fresh thyme and serve immediately.

COLORADO LAMB LOIN ON RATATOUILLE COULIS, TOPPED WITH GREEN ONIONS AND MERLOT SAUCE

HUBERT KELLER

Meat, tomato, wine, and stock are frequently encountered in classical French cuisine and are a familiar and reliable combination of basic and synergizing umami for countless preparations. Here, Hubert uses umami as a savory base for a lively, contemporary preparation that includes lots of healthful vegetables and a minimum of fat.

SERVES 4

FOR THE LAMB

2   **lamb loins** or rib eyes from 2 racks, trimmed
       to about 10 ounces each

1   tablespoon olive oil

4   sprigs fresh thyme

FOR THE RATATOUILLE COULIS

6   teaspoons olive oil

½   small shiny, firm eggplant (about ½ pound), diced ¼-inch
       Salt and freshly ground black pepper

2   small (1-inch diameter) green or yellow zucchini, diced ¼-inch

1   small sweet, firm **red bell pepper**, cored, seeded, and
       diced ¼-inch

1   small onion, minced

1   clove garlic, minced

1   small ripe **tomato**, peeled, seeded, and diced ¼-inch

½   teaspoon minced fresh thyme leaves

4 or 5 fresh basil leaves, finely sliced

FOR THE GREEN ONION COMPOTE

4½ teaspoons olive oil

18 scallions, white and tender green part only,
       cut diagonally ¼-inch-thick

4½ teaspoons heavy cream

FOR COOKING AND FINISHING THE LAMB

    Salt and freshly ground black pepper

2   tablespoons olive oil

1   medium onion, diced medium

1   medium **carrot**, peeled and diced medium

2   cloves garlic, crushed

½   cup **merlot wine**

1½ cups **Brown Chicken Stock** (page 79)

1½ teaspoons cornstarch

TO MARINATE THE LAMB: Place one lamb loin on a large piece of plastic wrap and brush with ½ tablespoon olive oil. Rub half the fresh thyme between your fingers to bruise it and release the oils, then rub the thyme on the lamb. Enclose the lamb and thyme tightly in the plastic wrap. Repeat with the second lamb loin. Refrigerate for at least 6 hours, or preferably overnight.

TO MAKE THE RATATOUILLE COULIS: In a medium nonstick skillet over medium heat, place 1½ teaspoons of the oil. Sauté the eggplant until soft, about 2 minutes. Season with salt and pepper and transfer to a mixing bowl. Add another 1½ teaspoons of the oil and sauté the zucchini until soft; season, and transfer to the bowl. Add another 1½ teaspoons of the oil and sauté the bell pepper until soft; season, and transfer. Finally, in the same pan with the remaining 1½ teaspoons oil, sauté the onion until light golden color, 2 to 3 minutes. Add the garlic and tomatoes to the pan. Lower the heat and simmer uncovered for 3 minutes. Add back the sautéed eggplant, zucchini, and bell pepper, and toss gently over moderate heat for 5 minutes. Stir in the minced thyme and the basil. Adjust the seasoning. Transfer to a blender and blend until very smooth. Reserve.

TO MAKE THE GREEN ONION COMPOTE: Heat the olive oil in a skillet and sauté the scallions over medium-high heat for 2 to 3 minutes, until just barely tender. Add the cream, season with salt and pepper, and continue cooking until the cream thickens, about 3 or 4 minutes. Adjust the seasoning and reserve.

TO COOK AND FINISH THE LAMB:

1. Preheat the oven to 425 degrees F.

2. Remove the lamb loins from the plastic wrap and season with salt and pepper. Heat 2 tablespoons olive oil in a large, heavy, ovenproof skillet over high heat. Add the lamb and sear both sides, about 2 minutes per side. Remove and reserve.

3. Place the onion, carrot, garlic, and the thyme from the lamb in the same skillet and sauté over medium-high heat for 3 minutes. Place the seared lamb back on top of the vegetables. Transfer the skillet to the oven for 7 to 8 minutes for medium rare.

4. Remove from the oven and place the lamb on a small plate inverted on a large plate, so the juices run off and the lamb stays crisp. Cover with aluminum foil and keep warm. Return the skillet and vegetables to the stove top and add the wine. Reduce over high heat until almost dry. Combine the Brown Chicken Stock and cornstarch in a bowl, add to the skillet and bring to a boil. Lower the heat to medium and reduce by half. Strain into a nonstick sauté pan. Add the lamb juices from the plate and simmer for 2 minutes. Adjust seasoning.

TO SERVE: Reheat the ratatouille coulis and spoon 1 to 2 tablespoons of it in the center of each warm dinner plate. Spread the coulis into a 4-inch circle. Slice each lamb loin into 4 equal slices, and top each slice with about 1 teaspoon of green onion compote. Place 2 slices of lamb in the center of the coulis. Spoon the merlot sauce all around between the ratatouille coulis and the edge of the plate. Serve immediately.

BROWN CHICKEN STOCK MAKES ABOUT 2 CUPS

1½ pounds **chicken bones**, plus 2 **chicken drumsticks**,
     roughly chopped

    Vegetable oil

1   small onion, diced medium

1   small **carrot**, peeled and diced medium

1   stalk celery, diced medium

1   small bay leaf (optional)

1   sprig thyme (optional)

Preheat the oven to 375 degrees F. Toss chicken bones and drumsticks in oil to coat. In a large roasting pan, roast chicken for 40 minutes. Add the onion, carrot, and celery, and roast for 20 minutes longer. Transfer to a stock pot and add the bay leaf and thyme (if using). Cover with cold water. Simmer uncovered for 2 to 2½ hours, skimming occasionally as needed. Strain and cool.

LAMB SHANKS WITH TOMATOES

CHRISTOPHER KIMBALL

In this updated version of an enduring classic, Chris set out to improve the taste profile with the addition of orange juice. Chris says "the sweet of the citrus tones the acid notes of the tomato, and ultimately adds a level of richness to the dish," because with a little less acid and a touch more sweetness, the umami is in better balance as well.

From Chris: Shanks are notorious for varying cooking times. The timing depends on the size of the shank. A thick one may take up to 2 hours; a small shank may only require 1 to 1½ hours. The meat should be very tender, literally falling off the bone. For a less fatty sauce, prepare this dish the day before, refrigerate the sauce separately from the shanks, and remove the congealed layer of fat. Combine the shanks and defatted sauce and reheat gently. Lamb shanks are not always easy to find and are best ordered in advance. Ask the butcher to cut them into sections for you.

SERVES 4

4	tablespoons olive oil, plus additional if necessary
4	pounds **lamb shanks**, cut into 1½- to 2-inch sections
2	medium onions, diced medium
5	cloves garlic, minced
1	cup dry **white wine**
1	(14- to 15-ounce) can **Italian plum tomatoes**, drained
¼	cup freshly squeezed orange juice
1	cup **chicken stock**
2	teaspoons fresh rosemary leaves, or 1 teaspoon dried
2	teaspoons fresh thyme leaves, or 1 teaspoon dried
2	teaspoons fresh marjoram leaves, or 1 teaspoon dried
¼	teaspoon ground cloves
1	bay leaf
1	teaspoon **balsamic vinegar**
1	teaspoon sugar
	Salt and freshly ground black pepper
4	small waxy **potatoes**, quartered (optional)

1. Preheat the oven to 200 degrees F.

2. Heat 2 tablespoons of the oil in large casserole or Dutch oven over medium-high heat. Brown the shanks on all sides in batches—do not overcrowd pan—adding more oil if necessary. Reserve the browned shanks in a bowl.

3. Add the remaining 2 tablespoons oil to the pan. Reduce the heat to medium. Add the onions and cook for 5 minutes. Add the garlic and cook until softened, about 1 minute. Turn heat to high, add the wine, and cook for 2 minutes, scraping the bottom of pan with a wooden spoon.

4. Stir in the tomatoes, orange juice, chicken stock, rosemary, thyme, marjoram, cloves, bay leaf, vinegar, and sugar. Season with salt and pepper to taste, and then return shanks to the pan along with any accumulated juices. Bring to a simmer, cover, and cook in oven for 1 hour. Add the potatoes, if using, and cook until shanks are tender and potatoes are done, at least 2 hours more.

5. Remove pan from oven, take out the lamb, potatoes, and bay leaf, skim off the fat, and puree the juices and vegetables. Return the meat and potatoes to the pot. Check seasonings and serve.

“Lamb shanks and veal shanks are my foundation recipes—a terrific foundation for interesting flavors.”

—CHRISTOPHER KIMBALL

OYSTER STEW WITH DRY SHERRY

CHRISTOPHER KIMBALL

Chris Kimball tells us, "The best oyster stew I ever tasted was at a luncheon at Julia Child's home in Cambridge, Massachusetts. The oysters were plump and just barely cooked. The milky broth was warm and buttery, a nice contrast to the briny oysters. This is my version of that dish. She served her stew with some grilled peasant bread. I suggest you do the same, even if you have to toast the store-bought variety."

Chris shares this simple, no-fuss oyster stew that leans heavily on just two umami ingredients to achieve a rather stellar eating experience—proof that piling on lots of umami ingredients may be nice, but is not necessary.

He reminds us that you must avoid overcooking the oysters. They will shrink and toughen. Make sure diners are on their way to the table before finishing this soup, as it is at its peak for a very short time.

SERVES 4 AS A MAIN COURSE OR 6 AS A FIRST COURSE

24	**oysters**
1	tablespoon olive oil
3	tablespoons butter
1	medium onion, peeled and diced
2	cups whole milk
2	cups light cream
1	tablespoon dry **sherry**
	Salt and freshly ground black pepper to taste
¼	cup minced flat-leaf parsley
	Hot sauce, for serving

1. Shuck the oysters (or have them shucked by your fishmonger—but they should be cooked soon after shucking) over a bowl. Strain the oyster liquor through cheesecloth and reserve.

2. In a pot large enough to comfortably hold all the ingredients, heat the olive oil and 1 tablespoon of butter over medium-high heat. When butter has stopped foaming, add the diced onion, reduce the heat to medium-low, and cook until tender, about 12 minutes.

3. Add the milk, cream, sherry, and strained oyster liquor. Bring to a boil, then reduce heat to a simmer.

4. Meanwhile, heat the remaining 2 tablespoons butter in a skillet and sauté oysters until plump and edges curl, about 2 minutes. Add to the simmering milk mixture.

5. Season with salt and pepper to taste. Cook for 4 to 5 minutes and serve in bowls garnished with the parsley. Hot sauce should be placed on the table.

JAPANESE PUMPKIN SOUP WITH SPICED CANDIED PECANS

JAKE KLEIN

This is an intensely flavored vegan soup that piles on layers of basic umami from the kabocha squash, kombu, and mirin (sweet rice wine vinegar). Jake likes to use orange-colored vegetables like winter squashes and carrots because "they stick to your tongue," contributing to the long finish that is a hallmark of umami.

SERVES 6 TO 8 AS A FIRST COURSE

FOR THE SPICED CANDIED PECANS

1   cup halved pecans

¼   cup sugar

1½ teaspoons salt

1   tablespoon shichimi togarashi (Japanese seven-spice powder),
       or 1 teaspoon cayenne pepper

FOR THE PUMPKIN SOUP

1   kabocha squash (Japanese pumpkin), about 3 pounds
       Salt and freshly ground white pepper

1   large Spanish onion, diced ½-inch (about 1½ cups)

1   (6-inch) piece **kombu** sea vegetable

1   quart purified water, or as needed

¼   cup **mirin**, or to taste

2   tablespoons grapeseed oil

3 to 4 scallions, thinly sliced on the bias

3 to 4 teaspoons toasted sesame oil

TO CANDY THE PECANS: In a nonreactive saucepan over medium heat, combine the pecans, sugar, salt, and shichimi togarashi. Cook while stirring until all of the sugar melts and the mixture starts to clump together. Remove from the heat, and spread to cool on a nonstick baking mat or lightly greased baking sheet. Once cooled, roughly chop the nuts. If not using directly, store in an airtight container.

TO MAKE THE SOUP:

1.   Preheat the oven to 350 degrees F. Cut the squash in half. Scoop out the seeds, and season the inside with salt and white pepper. Roast on a cookie sheet cut side down for approximately 30 minutes, until tender. Allow the pumpkin to cool until it can be handled comfortably.

2.   Scoop out the flesh of the roasted pumpkin. In a large, heavy saucepan over high heat, combine the roasted pumpkin, onion, kombu, and 3 cups of the water. Season the soup with salt and pepper. Bring to a boil and skim any impurities that rise to the top. Reduce the heat to a simmer, and cook until the onion is translucent, about 6 to 8 minutes. Remove from the heat and allow to cool slightly.

3.   While still warm, puree the soup in batches in a blender, adding the grapeseed oil and sufficient water to achieve the correct consistency: It should barely coat the back of a spoon. Season with mirin, salt, and white pepper.

TO SERVE: Reheat the soup gently in a nonreactive saucepan. Pour approximately ½ to ¾ cup of hot soup into each bowl. In the center of the bowl gently float a generous pinch of chopped scallions. Place about ½ to 1 tablespoon candied pecans on top of the scallions, and drizzle with ½ teaspoon sesame oil per bowl. Serve immediately.

WARM TOFU WITH SAIKYO MISO, ROASTED CASHEW, AND CHILI

JAKE KLEIN

No doubt due to the time he spent cooking in Hong Kong, Jake Klein's sense of umami is instinctive, unforced, and seamlessly integrated into his overall approach to cooking. "I don't think about umami when I create a recipe," he says. Nonetheless, his creations invariably include it, but always in balance with other tastes, and with a palate sensitive to harmony among tastes, aromas, and textures.

This dish combines one subtle umami source (heated tofu), one moderate (egg yolk) and one that is bolder (Saikyo miso, a version of white miso). These and other ingredients also contribute delicate sweet and salty notes, as well as two layers of heat from scallions and red chili. The broad range of textures derives from the creamy sauce, the soft tofu, the firmness of the garnishing vegetables, and the crunch of chopped nuts.

The sauce itself is an Asian-driven version of the sabayon used as the base of French hollandaise and the celebrated Italian dessert custard zabaglione.

SERVES 6 AS AN APPETIZER

1	box (1 pound) Japanese firm **tofu**
¼	cup **Saikyo miso** (see Sources, page 194)
1	**egg yolk**
1	teaspoon toasted sesame oil
¼	cup chopped, roasted cashews
4	teaspoons very thin scallion rings, green part only
1	teaspoon sliced red chili

1. Cut the block of tofu into 6 equal pieces. (You can do this by slicing the block in half lengthwise, and slicing it into thirds widthwise.) Place the tofu in a steamer basket positioned over simmering water to heat.

2. In a nonreactive bowl positioned over a saucepan of simmering water, whisk together the miso, egg yolk, sesame oil, and ⅓ cup water. Whisk about 10 minutes, until the mixture has thickened to the consistency of reduced heavy cream. The sauce should be rich, creamy, and salty-sweet.

3. To serve, place one block of tofu in the center of each plate. Spoon approximately 1 tablespoon sauce directly over the top of the block, allowing it to drip down the sides. Sprinkle each serving equally with the roasted cashews, scallion slices, and chili. Serve immediately.

CILANTRO SOUP WITH MONKFISH

NOBU MATSUHISA

In typical Nobu fashion—combining deep tradition and leaps of imagination—this refreshing soup uses a base of dashi, a fundamental preparation in Japanese cuisine. "The combination of kombu [pictured, right] and bonito makes a strong umami taste. It is a synergistic effect between the glutamate in kombu and inosinate (IMP) from bonito flakes. The Japanese have been using this recipe for centuries. This is my favorite umami combination," says Nobu.

From there, Nobu builds umami further with sake, soy sauce, and monkfish. He flavors the stock with the bright, fresh tang of cilantro and adds a subtle surprise with the gentle crispness of the deep–fried monkfish. Nobu reminds you to "make sure you add the monkfish when it is freshly fried and still hot."

The menegi used for garnish is an onion sprout native to Kyoto. Chives provide a similar effect and are easier to find.

SERVES 4 AS A FIRST COURSE

2¼ cups	**Nobu's Dashi** (opposite)
2	teaspoons **sake**
2	teaspoons light **soy sauce**
	Sea salt
9	ounces **monkfish**
	Freshly ground black pepper
	Vegetable oil, for deep-frying
	Arrowroot, for dusting
1	teaspoon finely chopped cilantro leaves
	Menegi or chives, for garnish
	Thin slices of lime, for garnish

1. Bring the dashi to a boil in a medium saucepan over high heat. Add the sake and soy sauce, and adjust the taste with about ¼ teaspoon sea salt.

2. Slice the monkfish into pieces about ½-inch thick and sprinkle with a little sea salt and black pepper.

3. Heat about 3 inches of oil in a medium saucepan to 340 to 350 degrees F. Dust the monkfish pieces with arrowroot and deep-fry for 3 to 4 minutes until crisp. Drain on paper towels.

4. Arrange the monkfish pieces in 4 soup dishes. Add the cilantro to the soup and pour into the dishes. Garnish with menegi or chives and lime. Serve immediately.

NOBU'S DASHI MAKES ABOUT 2¼ CUPS

¼   ounce (about 20 square inches) **kombu** sea vegetable

⅔   ounce **dried bonito flakes** (katsuobushi)

     (about ¾ cup, packed tightly)

Slowly heat the kombu in 2½ cups water in a saucepan. Just before the water boils, remove the kombu (to prevent scum from forming), add the bonito flakes, and turn off the heat. After the bonito flakes sink to the bottom of the pan, strain the contents of the pan though a sieve lined with paper towel.

SPICY SOUR BOTAN SHRIMP

NOBU MATSUHISA

To connoisseurs of Japanese food, the combination of shrimp, mushrooms, and soy sauce is a familiar and comforting umami mixture that is light, nourishing, and deeply satisfying. Nobu's Spicy Sour Botan Shrimp is an easy-to-make dish with explosive flavors in which Nobu combines pungent chilis and garlic with tart and fruity lemon and sweet, succulent botan shrimp. The fermented bean paste flavored with garlic and chiles adds another umami dimension.

For genuine, giant botan shrimp, the kind served at Nobu's restaurants, seek out a fishmonger who supplies sushi restaurants, or use the freshest, biggest shrimp you can find, preferably nothing smaller than U-15 size. Nobu tells us that scallops, another potent umami source, are also delectable sautéed and served with Spicy Sour Sauce.

SERVES 4

8	fresh botan **shrimp** (about 1½ ounces each)
	Sea salt
	Freshly ground black pepper
1	broccoli floret, cut at stems into pieces
2	tablespoons clarified butter, store-bought or homemade (opposite)
½	cup **Spicy Sour Sauce** (opposite)
3½	ounces **enoki mushrooms** (about 1½ packages)
10	chive spears, cut into 1½-inch lengths

1. Prepare the shrimp by removing the heads (if needed), shelling, and deveining. Rinse briefly in cold water and drain. Sprinkle with a little sea salt and black pepper.

2. Bring a small pot of water to a boil and add a pinch of sea salt. Add the broccoli and boil for 90 seconds. Plunge briefly into ice water and drain.

3. Heat a wok or medium skillet over high heat. Add the butter and sauté the shrimp. When the shrimp turn opaque, add the Spicy Sour Sauce, broccoli, mushrooms, and chives, and stir-fry briefly.

4. Transfer to a serving dish.

SPICY SOUR SAUCE MAKES ABOUT ½ CUP

½   cup freshly squeezed lemon juice

1   teaspoon **fermented bean paste** flavored with garlic and chilis

½   teaspoon **light soy sauce**

½   teaspoon **soy sauce**

Combine all ingredients and mix well. Pass mixture through a fine sieve. Reserve hot until needed.

TO CLARIFY BUTTER: Heat 2 sticks (½ pound) unsalted butter in a small saucepan over medium heat for about 20 minutes, or until the butter separates into three distinct layers: foam on top, clear yellow liquid in the center, and white residue at the bottom. Skim and discard the foam. Pour the liquid and the residue into a coffee filter placed in a funnel over a bowl until the clear yellow liquid (which is the clarified butter) passes through, leaving the residue behind in the filter, which you discard. Store unused portion covered in the refrigerator for up to 3 weeks.

NOTE. Make this in a well-seasoned wok if you have one, or use a nonreactive skillet—not cast-iron or aluminum, which will discolor the food because of the lemon juice. Nobu specifies clarified butter because it withstands more heat. Whole butter will burn at stir-fry temperatures.

MARINATED SKIRT STEAK WITH AVOCADO-TOMATILLO DIPPING SAUCE

MARY SUE MILLIKEN AND SUSAN FENIGER

Although gaining in popularity—and, therefore, rising in price—skirt steak remains one of the tastiest, most affordable cuts of steak on the market. It delivers plenty of umami by itself, but when marinated with synergizing Worcestershire and soy sauce, it takes on an even richer, beefier character, further enhanced by the heat, salt, and sour of the other marinating ingredients and the dipping sauce.

Two cautions: First, don't add salt to the marinade or salt the beef before it goes in. There's already salt in the Worcestershire and soy sauce and adding more will draw juices out of the steak, producing meat that is drier than it needs to be. Second, cook the steaks on a very hot grill or skillet for only the time specified. They cook quickly and get tough fast if left on too long.

SERVES 6

3	cloves garlic, minced
2	teaspoons dry mustard
1	tablespoon **Worcestershire sauce**
3	tablespoons **soy sauce**
1	teaspoon Tabasco sauce
1	teaspoon freshly ground black pepper
1	tablespoon **red wine vinegar**
1	tablespoon freshly squeezed lemon juice
½	cup olive oil
3	pounds **skirt steak**, trimmed of excess fat
	Vegetable oil, for cooking
	Avocado-Tomatillo Dipping Sauce (opposite)
	Huitlacoche Quesadillas, for serving (page 94)

1. Place the garlic, mustard, Worcestershire sacue, soy sauce, Tabasco, pepper, vinegar, lemon juice, and oil in a blender and puree until smooth.

2. Cut the steak into 6 serving-size pieces. Generously slather the meat with the marinade and roll each piece up into a cylinder. Arrange the rolled steaks in a shallow pan and pour on the remaining marinade. Cover and marinate in the refrigerator for 6 to 12 hours.

3. About 30 minutes before cooking, remove the meat from the refrigerator. Unroll the steaks, remove excess marinade, and place the steaks on a platter.

4. Heat the grill or broiler to very hot, or lightly coat a cast-iron skillet with oil and heat it to very hot.

5. Cook the steaks just until seared on both sides, 3 to 4 minutes per side for medium rare. Transfer the cooked steaks to a cutting board and let rest for 3 to 5 minutes. Slice across the grain into diagonal strips.

6. Serve hot with Avocado-Tomatillo Dipping Sauce and Huitlacoche Quesadillas.

AVOCADO-TOMATILLO DIPPING SAUCE

1   pound tomatillos (8 to 10 tomatillos), husked, washed, and cut into quarters

2 to 4 large jalapeño peppers, stemmed, seeded if desired, and roughly chopped

½   cup freshly squeezed orange juice

3 to 4 scallions, white and light green parts only, roughly chopped

1   generous bunch cilantro, leaves and small stems only, roughly chopped (about 2 cups)

2   teaspoons salt

2   medium avocados, halved, pitted, and peeled

Place the tomatillos, jalapeños, and orange juice in a blender. Pulse just until chunky. Add the scallions, cilantro, salt, and avocados, and puree about 2 minutes more, until smooth.

HUITLACOCHE QUESADILLAS

MARY SUE MILLIKEN AND SUSAN FENIGER

Mary Sue Milliken and Susan Feniger have spent nearly three decades cooking and creating and managing successful restaurants. They have consistently startled us with un-expected culinary inventions that highlight the cuisines and customs of other cultures. But unlike some other visionary chefs, they aren't just daring us to eat their clever food, they are inviting us to broaden our horizons with novel and delicious foods that are original yet faithful to their roots. This recipe is a mouthwatering case in point.

Huitlacoche (weet-la-CO-chay) is what's left after the ordinary yellow kernels of sweet corn have been transformed by the fungus Ustilago maydis *into knurly, swollen black pods. Also called cuitlachoche, maize mushroom, and Mexican truffle, the fungus that causes huitlacoche is regarded as a disease in most of the world, rendering entire corn crops unmarketable. But in Mexico, an infestation of huitlacoche is a blessing as it turns an everyday staple into a sweet, smoky, mushroomy delicacy alive with flavor and both basic and synergizing umami.*

This easy-to-make recipe combines huitlacoche and three cheeses with various degrees of additional umami, together with piquant red onions and jalapeños. Panela is a mild, milky Mexican cheese similar in taste to an excellent and flavorful ricotta cheese, which desperate cooks may resort to in a pinch.

SERVES 6

5	tablespoons unsalted butter
½	cup finely diced red onion
2	jalapeño peppers, stemmed, seeded, and finely diced
1	pound **huitlacoche**, roughly chopped (see Sources, page 194)
1	teaspoon salt
½	teaspoon freshly ground black pepper
1½	cups grated **manchego** or Monterey Jack cheese
1	cup grated panela cheese
½	cup grated **anejo**, **Parmesan**, or **pecorino Romano** cheese
6	flour tortillas

1. Melt 3 tablespoons of the butter in a medium skillet over medium heat. Cook the onions and jalapeños until soft, about 5 minutes. Stir in the huitlacoche, salt and pepper. Reduce the heat to low and cook, stirring frequently, until the mixture is aromatic and wilted, about 5 minutes more. Set aside.

2. Preheat the oven to 350 degrees F.

3. In a bowl, combine the 3 cheeses. Lay the tortillas out on a counter. Divide the cheese mixture into 6 portions and arrange one portion over half of each tortilla. Divide the vegetable mixture into 6 portions and sprinkle evenly over the cheese. Fold over each tortilla to enclose the filling.

4. Melt the remaining 2 tablespoons butter in a very small saucepan over low heat, or in a small ramekin in the microwave.

5. Place a dry griddle or cast-iron skillet over medium-high heat. Brush one side of a quesadilla with melted butter and place buttered side down in the pan. Cook until very light golden, about 1 minute. Then brush the uncoated side with butter and flip over. Cook until the other side is light golden and transfer to a baking sheet. When all the quesadillas are browned, transfer the baking sheet to the oven and bake 10 minutes, until the cheeses begin to ooze. Serve hot, whole or cut into wedges.

WHOLE FISH BRAISED WITH TOMATOES, CAPERS, OLIVES, AND HERBS (*page 62*)

. *chef* RICK BAYLESS .

above . ASPARAGUS SALAD WITH ROASTED PEPPERS AND SHAVED PARMIGIANO-REGGIANO (*page 70*)
. *chef* GARY DANKO .

left . SEA SCALLOPS WITH MASHED POTATOES AND RED ONION CONFIT (*page 68*)
. *chef* DANIEL BOULUD .

above . WILD MUSHROOMS IN A POTATO SHELL ACCENTED WITH CARAMELIZED VEGETABLE JUS (*page 74*)

. *chef* HUBERT KELLER .

right . LAMB SHANKS WITH TOMATOES (*page 80*)

. *chef* CHRISTOPHER KIMBALL .

above . MARINATED SKIRT STEAK WITH AVOCADO-TOMATILLO DIPPING SAUCE (*page 92*)

. *chefs* MARY SUE MILLIKEN AND SUSAN FENIGER .

right . SPICY SOUR BOTAN SHRIMP (*page 90*)

. *chef* NOBU MATSUHISA .

GREEN BEAN TEMPURA WITH ASIAN DIPPING SAUCE (*page 114*)
. *chef* PATRICK O'CONNELL .

CORNISH GAME HENS BRAISED IN A POT WITH SUMMER VEGETABLES (*page 122*)

. *chef* BRADLEY OGDEN .

above . TRUFFLED MAC AND CHEESE (*page 132*)

. *chef* JON PRATT .

left . ROAST PORK SHOULDER WITH WHITE BEANS, SMOKED BACON, AND KALE (*page 120*)

. *chef* BRADLEY OGDEN .

above . LOBSTER AVGOLEMONO (*page 146*)

. *chef* LYDIA SHIRE .

left . WOOD-GRILLED RIB STEAK WITH SHIITAKE-WINE SAUCE (*page 138*)

. *chef* STEVEN RAICHLEN .

above . MY FATHER'S FAMOUS SHRIMP HORS D'OEUVRES (*page 144*)

. *chef* LYDIA SHIRE .

right . PEA CAKES WITH TOMATO SALSA (*page 150*)

. *chef* FRANK STITT .

DEEP-FRIED SUSHI WITH WASABI MISO (*page 174*)

. *chef* NORMAN VAN AKEN .

GREEN BEAN TEMPURA WITH ASIAN DIPPING SAUCE

PATRICK O'CONNELL

Patrick O'Connell works with umami the way a great composer works with instruments in an orchestra. "I know umami instinctively," he says. In fact, Patrick often uses analogies to music when describing his food. "When I taste something I like, my hand slowly stretches outward, indicating long, lingering notes," which, more often than not, means umami is at work. "For me, umami triggers a chord that goes on and on, like it's never over."

Patrick proves his point in his delectably unassuming Green Bean Tempura with Asian Dipping Sauce, a testament to the virtues of simplicity. The nuoc mam fish sauce delivers synergizing umami, exposing the otherwise subtle basic umami in the green beans. "We use the long, thin, French green beans and present them in a silver cup, lined with a parchment paper cone," he says. You needn't be as formal. In fact, these quick and easy finger foods, cooked in small batches and served immediately, are the perfect way to keep guests gathered around in the kitchen munching happily until dinner is ready to go on the table.

SERVES 4

2 quarts vegetable or peanut oil, for deep frying

½ pound French **green beans**

Tempura Batter (opposite)

Salt to taste

Clear Fish Sauce with Lime and Cilantro (opposite)

1. In a deep fryer or heavy pot, heat the oil to 350 degrees F.

2. Cut off the tips of the green beans.

3. Dip each green bean into the Tempura Batter and shake off any excess. Carefully drop each bean into the hot oil and fry for about 90 seconds, turning them with a slotted spoon until they are just golden and crisp.

4. Remove the beans from the fryer and drain them on paper towels. Season with salt and serve immediately, with the Clear Fish Sauce on the side.

TEMPURA BATTER

Chef O'Connell notes, "After years of experimenting with every tempura batter imaginable, we finally discovered that, oftentimes, simpler is better. This recipe uses only soda water, flour, salt, and pepper. Fine-textured soft-wheat flour, packaged as cake flour, makes a more delicate tempura, but regular flour will suffice."

1   cup cake flour
7   fluid ounces (1 cup less 2 tablespoons) very cold club soda
    Salt and freshly ground black pepper

1. Using a fork, gently combine the flour and club soda in a small bowl. (The batter will appear slightly lumpy and should have the consistency of heavy cream.)

2. Season with salt and pepper to taste. (The bubbles in the soda water help keep the tempura light and crispy; therefore it is important to make the batter just before using it.)

CLEAR FISH SAUCE WITH LIME AND CILANTRO

1   tablespoon **rice wine vinegar**
7   tablespoons **nuoc mam** (Vietnamese fish sauce)
2   tablespoons sugar
½   cup cold water
     Juice of 1 lime
2   tablespoons finely julienned **carrot**
¼   cup minced fresh cilantro
2   large cloves garlic, minced
2   jalapeño peppers, ribs and seeds removed, finely chopped

Mix all the ingredients together in a medium bowl, stirring until the sugar is dissolved. Store in the refrigerator until ready to use.

FIRE AND ICE: SEARED PEPPERED TUNA WITH DAIKON RADISH AND CUCUMBER SORBET

PATRICK O'CONNELL

An umami staple in Asian cuisine, the combination of soy sauce, fish sauce, rice wine vinegar, and tuna is at this recipe's foundation. But rather than seeming familiar, Patrick's creation is completely original and full of delightful surprises.

He says, "The spicy heat of the seared, peppered tuna, which is still raw in the center, is intriguingly juxtaposed with an intensely flavored, icy and refreshing cucumber sorbet. The tuna is mounded on a little nest of dressed vermicelli and garnished with cucumber salsa. While this dish may initially strike you as strange or unapproachable, it is neither. If you don't have time to make the cucumber sorbet, the tuna will still be delicious without it."

Patrick shows how a sturdy base of umami lets him build flavors, textures, even temperatures, to startling heights, and still create a dish with unquestionable integrity and a profoundly memorable dining experience. For Patrick, umami is a device that lets him "take something ephemeral and make it permanent."

SERVES 6

FOR THE VERMICELLI NOODLES

3   tablespoons **soy sauce**

1   teaspoon nuoc mam (Vietnamese **fish sauce**)

2   tablespoons **rice wine vinegar**

1   teaspoon sugar

2   teaspoons peanut oil

1   tablespoon mustard seeds

¼   cup thinly sliced red onion

2   tablespoons chopped fresh cilantro leaves

2   ounces vermicelli rice noodles or angel hair pasta

FOR THE SOY DRESSING FOR THE TUNA

1   cup **soy sauce**

¼   cup **rice wine vinegar**

¼   cup sugar

¾   cup finely grated fresh daikon radish

FOR THE PEPPERED TUNA

2   tablespoons black peppercorns

½   pound very fresh **tuna loin** in 1 piece

1   teaspoon vegetable oil

      Cilantro leaves, for garnish

½   cup Cucumber Salsa (page 118)

1   cup Cucumber Sorbet (page 119)

TO PREPARE THE VERMICELLI:

1. In a mixing bowl, combine the soy sauce, nuoc mam, vinegar, sugar, peanut oil, mustard seeds, red onion, and cilantro leaves and reserve.

2. In a large pot, bring 2 quarts of salted water to a boil. Add the vermicelli and cook for 2 to 3 minutes, until the noodles are al dente. Drain the noodles, rinse them with cold water and add them to the soy sauce mixture. The noodles may be made ahead and refrigerated until ready to serve.

TO MAKE THE SOY DRESSING FOR THE TUNA: In a small mixing bowl, combine the soy sauce, vinegar, sugar, and daikon radish. This may be made several days ahead and refrigerated.

TO SEAR THE TUNA:

1. Place the peppercorns on a wooden cutting board and crack them coarsely with a meat pounder or the bottom of a small, heavy saucepan. Press the cracked peppercorns onto both sides of the tuna.

2. In a cast-iron skillet, heat the oil over high heat until smoking. Sear the tuna for 45 seconds on each side. Transfer the tuna to a cutting board and slice it into ⅛-inch-thick slices.

TO SERVE: In each of 6 serving bowls, place a few tablespoons of soy dressing. Arrange a small mound of vermicelli noodles in the center of each bowl.

Fan 4 or 5 slices of tuna over the noodles and garnish with cilantro leaves. Place 1 tablespoon of Cucumber Salsa and a small scoop of Cucumber Sorbet on top of the tuna.

CUCUMBER SALSA MAKES ABOUT 2 CUPS

½   large European seedless cucumber, peeled and finely diced

4½   teaspoons finely chopped fresh dill

2   teaspoons finely diced jalapeño pepper

1   tablespoon finely diced red onion

2   tablespoons **rice wine vinegar**

Pinch of salt

Sugar to taste

In a mixing bowl combine the cucumber, dill, jalapeño, onion, vinegar, salt, and sugar to taste. Refrigerate until ready to use.

CUCUMBER SORBET MAKES ABOUT 1½ QUARTS

2½ large European seedless cucumbers, not peeled

¾ cup light corn syrup

½ cup sugar

½ cup freshly squeezed lemon juice

1 teaspoon salt

¼ cup minced fresh dill

2 tablespoons citron-flavored vodka

2 **egg whites**

1. Using a blender or food processor, puree the cucumbers (you should have about 4 cups). Strain through a fine-mesh sieve.

2. Add the corn syrup, sugar, lemon juice, salt, dill, and vodka to the cucumber juice.

3. Whisk the egg whites until frothy and stir them into the cucumber mixture. Freeze in an ice cream machine according to the manufacturer's instructions. Store in the freezer in a closed container until ready to use.

ROAST PORK SHOULDER WITH WHITE BEANS, SMOKED BACON, AND KALE

BRADLEY OGDEN

Here is a savory variation on good, old-fashioned pork and beans. Searing and then slow-cooking the pork butt with beans and a medley of veggies promotes development of maximum umami from all ingredients. The result is a veritable symphony of basic and synergizing umami components harmonized with an array of aromas, textures, and other tastes.

Note that this is cooked in several stages, ensuring that each ingredient is cooked properly and presented at the peak of flavor and texture.

SERVES 4

2	pounds boneless **pork butt**
1	teaspoon freshly cracked black pepper
1	teaspoon kosher salt
2	tablespoons olive oil
2	ounces smoked **slab bacon**, sliced ¼-inch thick
2	stalks celery, cut into 2- to 3-inch pieces
2	small **carrots**, peeled and cut into 2- to 3-inch pieces
½	medium onion, chopped
4	small cloves garlic, crushed
6	sprigs fresh thyme, or ½ teaspoon dried
1	bay leaf
½	cup small **white beans**, soaked overnight in cold water and drained
1½	cups **chicken stock** or **broth**
2	teaspoons **red wine vinegar**
1	cup chopped **tomatoes**
6	ounces fresh kale, collards, or mustard greens, washed, stemmed, and coarsely chopped (about 1½ cups, tightly packed)

1.   Trim the outside fat from the pork butt to ⅛-inch thick. Tie the meat with string to make a compact piece that will not fall apart while cooking.

2.   Cut the bacon across to make ¼ by ¼ by 1-inch pieces.

3.   Season the pork with ½ teaspoon each pepper and salt. Place 1 tablespoon of the olive oil in a heavy, ovenproof saucepan over high heat. Sear the meat on all sides. Remove and set aside.

4.   Pour excess fat out of the pan, leaving about 1 tablespoon. Reduce heat to medium. Add the bacon to the pan and cook until golden brown and slightly crispy. Add the celery, carrots, onions, 2 of the garlic cloves, thyme, and bay leaf. Sauté for 4 to 5 minutes. Add the beans, stock, red wine vinegar, and ¾ cup water. Bring to a simmer, reduce heat, cover, and cook for 30 to 40 minutes, until the beans are tender. You may need to add water during the cooking if the tops of the beans begin to dry out.

5.   Preheat the oven to 375 degrees F.

6.   Finely mince the remaining 2 cloves of garlic. In a medium sauté pan heat the remaining tablespoon olive oil over medium heat. Add the garlic and cook for only 1 minute, being careful not to brown. Add the tomatoes and cook for 2 to 3 minutes until the tomatoes begin to render their juice. Add the kale. Cook for 4 to 5 minutes longer, until the kale is wilted. Remove from the heat and set aside.

7.   When the beans have finished cooking, remove the carrots, celery, and thyme sprigs. Add the tomato and kale mixture. Stir in the remaining ½ teaspoon each of salt and pepper. Place the browned pork butt on top of the beans along with any juices that may have collected, cover, and bake for 40 minutes to 1 hour, until the meat is very tender. Check the pan and add more liquid if the beans are drying out.

8.   Remove from the oven and allow to rest in the pan for 5 to 10 minutes. Untie the roast and slice ¼-inch thick. Spoon out the bean, tomato, and kale mixture onto warm plates or a serving platter. Place the meat on the beans and serve with any remaining liquid in the pan.

CORNISH GAME HENS BRAISED IN A POT WITH SUMMER VEGETABLES

BRADLEY OGDEN

Braising is often reserved for tougher cuts of meat (see Bradley's pork and beans recipe, page 120). But Cornish game hens are naturally tender and somewhat delicate, so the cooking time is greatly reduced. Yet even short-cooked braising like this allows all the flavors—the hens, vegetables, aromatics, and herbs—to mingle and develop richness in a way not possible with roasted birds served with vegetables on the side. The shorter cooking time also means the vegetables remain fully intact, so their flavors are more distinct and their textures more substantial than in long-cooked braises.

The umami formula is a simple, straightforward one of hens, potatoes, salt pork, and shiitake mushrooms, truly the transforming ingredient. Leave out the shiitakes and the fifth taste dimension is seriously diminished, and with it, the enjoyment of the other ingredients.

SERVES 4

2	**Cornish game hens**, 1¼ to 1½ pounds each, wing tips removed
1	teaspoon kosher salt
1	teaspoon freshly cracked black pepper
1	teaspoon minced garlic
4	sprigs fresh tarragon, or ½ teaspoon dried
8	small red new **potatoes**
¼	cup olive oil
2	ounces **salt pork**, sliced very thin or frozen and shaved into thin slices
4	medium **carrots**, peeled and cut on the bias into 3-inch pieces
8	small boiling onions, peeled
4	whole cloves garlic

½ bay leaf

4 sprigs fresh thyme, or ¼ teaspoon dried

2 sprigs fresh summer savory, or ¼ teaspoon dried

2 cups **chicken stock** or **broth**

2 teaspoons **white wine vinegar** or **tarragon vinegar**

8 **shiitake mushroom** caps, wiped with a damp cloth

1. Preheat the oven to 350 degrees F.

2. Rub the cavity of each hen with ½ teaspoon each of salt, pepper, and minced garlic. Place 2 sprigs of tarragon (or ¼ teaspoon dried) in each bird and tie the drumsticks together.

3. Rinse the potatoes in cold water and peel a thin spiral ribbon of skin from each potato.

4. Heat the olive oil over medium-high heat in a Dutch oven, heavy covered skillet, or cast-iron pan with a lid, large enough to hold both birds. Add the birds and sear on all sides. After 5 minutes add the salt pork and continue cooking until hens are well browned. Add the carrots, onions, potatoes, and whole garlic cloves, and cook for 2 minutes to slightly caramelize them.

5. Add the bay leaf, thyme, savory, chicken stock, and vinegar, and bring to a simmer. Cover the pot and place in the oven. After 15 minutes, add the mushrooms. Continue to braise, covered, for 5 more minutes, or until the hens are tender.

6. Remove the vegetables, herb sprigs, and hens to a serving platter and keep warm. Discard the bay leaf and skim the fat from the juices in the pot. Place the pot over high heat, bring the juices to a boil, and reduce for several minutes.

7. Season to taste. Cut the hens in half, pour the juices over the vegetables, and serve.

HAMACHI WITH EXOTIC SPICED SASSAFRAS GLAZE AND BONITO

KEN ORINGER

Ken Oringer has built a reputation for edgy creations using an assortment of exotic ingredients. This dish is centered on a sassafras glaze and seasoned with grains of paradise (peppery with hints of ginger and cardamom), long pepper (a touch spicier than black pepper), and shichimi togarashi (Japanese seven-spice powder). All are available online (see Sources, page 194), as are the other unusual ingredients.

Ken starts with a sturdy base of umami, in this case a fairly familiar Asian concoction of tuna, dashi, soy sauce, and bonito. He then creates layers of pleasing, complementary flavors, each of which remains distinct, memorable, and substantial thanks to the umami foundation.

In spite of its delicate appearance, this is a moving food experience.

SERVES 4 FOR DINNER

FOR THE SASSAFRAS GLAZE

1   pound fresh sassafras root, chipped

½   cup sugar

½   teaspoon **hon dashi** (powdered dashi boullion)

    Soy sauce to taste

    Shichimi togarashi to taste

FOR THE FISH

1   piece Japanese **yellowtail**, cut into a 6 by 1½
    by 1½-inch block

    Sea salt

    Grains of paradise, cracked

    Ground long pepper

    Maldon sea salt

1   cup **bonito** flakes, preferably shaved fresh

2   ounces micro shiso

1   cup lemon puree (canned or thawed if frozen)

1   cup pickled spruce buds

½   cup daylily flower buds

1.   In a medium pot, combine the sassafras, sugar, dashi, and 2 quarts water. Simmer for 1 hour. Let infuse overnight. The next day, strain and reduce to a glaze, about ½ cup. Season to taste with soy sauce and shichimi togarashi.

2.   Heat a grill to medium. Slice the fish into 4 equal portions and season it with sea salt. Grill gently on both sides until warmed through. Rest fish briefly.

3.   Apply sassafras glaze with pastry brush. Season with grains of paradise, long pepper, and Maldon salt. Top with bonito flakes and shiso.

4.   Serve with lemon puree, pickled spruce buds, and daylily buds.

STEAMED BLACK BASS WITH HOT GARLIC OIL, THAI CHILI DIPPING SAUCE, AND CANDIED ORANGE RIND

KEN ORINGER

Ken uses just two umami sources, black bass and fermented Chinese black beans, efficiently combining basic and synergizing umami. But this is merely the savory canvas onto which he paints a rainbow of fruity, spicy notes supported by and enhancing the more deeply flavored bass and beans.

Ken points out that steaming in the oven, not on the stovetop, "combines wet and dry heat, helping the fish develop more complex flavors."

SERVES 4 FOR DINNER

FOR THE CANDIED ORANGE RIND

1   orange

1   cup sugar

FOR THE THAI CHILI DIPPING SAUCE

¼   cup **soy sauce**

1   teaspoon grated ginger

1   tablespoon **rice wine vinegar**

1   tablespoon sesame oil

1   Thai chili, sliced very thin

FOR THE FISH

4   **black bass**, scaled, gutted, and filleted
     Salt and freshly ground black pepper

3   tablespoons unsalted butter, softened

1   tablespoon chopped fresh lemon zest

1   tablespoon chopped fresh orange zest

1   tablespoon chopped fresh lime zest

3   tablespoons finely sliced kaffir lime leaf

2   tablespoons chopped **Chinese black beans**

¼   cup garlic oil (homemade or store-bought)

2   tablespoons Korean pepper threads
     (available from Asian grocers)

2   bunches cilantro, stemmed and roughly chopped

TO MAKE THE CANDIED ORANGE RIND:

1.   Preheat the oven to 200 degrees F.

2.   Remove the orange rind using a vegetable peeler, making sure to leave behind all the white pith.

3.   Combine orange rind with cold water in a saucepan, bring to a boil, then drain. Repeat this process 5 times.

4.   In the same pan, combine the orange rind with 1 cup water and the sugar. Cook on low heat until orange rind becomes translucent, about 30 minutes. Transfer to a sheet pan lined with parchment paper. Dry in a 200 degree F oven for 2 to 3 hours or until crisp. Set aside in a tightly closed container until needed.

TO MAKE THE THAI CHILI DIPPING SAUCE: Combine the soy sauce, ginger, vinegar, sesame oil, and chili in a small bowl and mix well. Set aside until needed.

TO MAKE AND SERVE THE FISH:

1.   Preheat the oven to 400 degrees F.

2.   Set up a large bamboo steamer to accommodate all the fish. Season the fillets with salt and pepper. Rub with softened butter and place on a plate in one layer, skin side up. Scatter citrus zests, lime leaf, and black beans on top of the fish. Set aside in the refrigerator until needed.

3.   When ready to steam, put fish plate into steamer. Place steamer on bottom rack of the oven. Steam until just cooked, about 20 to 25 minutes.

4.   Meanwhile, heat garlic oil until smoking.

5.   When fish is done, use a slotted spatula to transfer to a serving platter. Mix the fish juices remaining in the dish with the chili dipping sauce. Pour over fish. Top with hot oil, Korean pepper threads, cilantro, and candied orange rind. Serve.

CRISP FLATTENED CHICKEN WITH BOULANGERIE POTATOES

MARK PEEL

According to Mark, "chicken with a brick" is the literal translation of the colloquial Italian name for this dish, pollo al mattone, which he first saw at a small, family-run restaurant in Tuscany. And while a paint can filled with cement was used to flatten the chicken in a hot cast-iron skillet when he saw it in Tuscany, Mark recommends weighing the chicken down with a second cast-iron skillet, just like the one used to cook the chicken. Don't cook the chicken in a nonstick pan; you will not be able to achieve the crispiness or deep browning characteristic of the dish. Also, he notes you should not crowd the pan. Finally, do not cook over high heat, or the chicken skin will burn before the meat is cooked.

Mark proves that for umami to make a big contribution to a dish, it need not be fancy and it need not be the featured attraction. Chicken, bacon, potatoes, mushrooms, and chicken stock are a familiar and nourishing umami combination that works as a foundation for Mark's two somewhat unusual techniques (pressing chicken in the pan and glazing potatoes with stock), which are the real stars of the show.

SERVES 2 TO 4

1   (3½-pound) **chicken**, split in half and boned (ask a butcher
     to do it if you don't know how)
4   large cloves garlic, sliced thin
2   tablespoons fresh marjoram leaves
     Kosher salt and freshly cracked black pepper
2   tablespoons vegetable oil
     Boulangerie Potatoes (opposite)

1. Carefully lift, but do not remove, the skin from the meat of each chicken half. Divide the garlic slices and marjoram leaves equally and stuff them under the skin of the chicken halves. Refrigerate, covered, for 2 to 3 hours.

2. Just before sautéing, season the chicken pieces lightly with salt and pepper.

3.   In a large cast-iron skillet over medium-high heat, heat the vegetable oil. When the oil is almost smoking, put the 2 halves of chicken in the skillet, skin side down. Place an unheated cast-iron skillet of the same size as the first on top, with the bottom pressing down on the chicken. Cook until the chicken is nicely browned and the skin is crispy, 12 to 15 minutes.

4.   Remove the top skillet and turn the chicken halves over. Cook uncovered until the underside loses its pink color, 6 to 7 minutes longer. Remove the chicken from the skillet.

5.   To serve, place the chicken halves on plates and spoon potatoes to the side. Serve immediately.

BOULANGERIE POTATOES SERVES 4 AS A SIDE DISH

1	tablespoon unsalted butter
1	medium white or yellow onion, sliced ¼-inch thick
2	thick slices **bacon**, cut into ¼ by ¼ by 1-inch lardons
1	pound Yukon gold or fingerling **potatoes**, diced large
1	tablespoon fresh thyme leaves
½	cup large-diced fresh **porcini mushrooms** (see Note)
½	cup **chicken stock** (1 cup if using dried porcinis)
	Kosher salt and freshly ground black pepper

Heat the butter in a large skillet set on medium and cook the onions until light brown. Add bacon and cook until browned. Add the potatoes, thyme, and porcini mushrooms. Add the chicken stock 2 tablespoons at a time, basting the potatoes. As the stock reduces, add more and continue basting until potatoes are cooked and glazed, about 20 minutes. Season to taste with salt and pepper. Keep warm until ready to serve.

N O T E .   If fresh porcini mushrooms are not available, use roughly ¼ cup (a small handful) dried porcini mushrooms instead. To reconstitute, combine the dried mushrooms with 1 cup chicken stock in small saucepan and bring to a boil. Remove from the heat and set aside until ready to use for potatoes. When ready to add mushrooms and stock to potatoes, carefully lift out the mushrooms and strain the stock. Make sure you have ½ cup of stock left. Some will evaporate and some will be absorbed by the mushrooms. Adjust if needed.

GRILLED SQUID SALAD WITH TOMATOES, OLIVES, AND CUCUMBERS IN AN OREGANO VINAIGRETTE

MARK PEEL

This is a simple, rustic, and intensely flavorful salad that will transport you to the sun-drenched Mediterranean in single bite. Mark has included generous helpings of basic and synergizing umami to impart the dish with savory satisfaction. But he has also balanced it with sweet from squid and tomatoes; a range of sour notes from tomatoes, vinegar, lemon juice, and olives; salt from olives and seasoning; even touches of bitter from the niçoise olives, oregano and charring from the grilled squid.

Be vigilant when grilling the squid. It cooks quickly and gets tough fast if you leave it on even a minute too long.

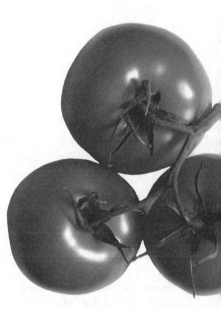

SERVES 4

2 teaspoons freshly squeezed lemon juice,
 plus additional if necessary

1 tablespoon **red wine vinegar**

2 teaspoons dried oregano

1 garlic clove, finely chopped (about 1 teaspoon)

¼ cup vegetable oil

¾ cup extra virgin olive oil

 Kosher salt

 Freshly cracked black pepper

2 medium cucumbers

½ pint cherry **tomatoes**

2½ pounds cleaned, whole **calamari**

½ cup pitted niçoise **olives**

1. In a bowl, whisk together the lemon juice, vinegar, oregano, garlic, vegetable oil, ¼ cup of the olive oil, and ¾ teaspoon salt. Season with more lemon juice, salt, and pepper to taste.

2. Cut the cucumbers in half lengthwise and remove the seeds. Slice into ¼-inch-thick slices. Slice the cherry tomatoes in half.

3. Heat a grill to high. Toss together the calamari, the remaining ½ cup olive oil, and salt and pepper to taste. Grill until firm in texture, 4 to 5 minutes, turning once. Slice the calamari bodies into ¼-inch-thick rings. Slice the tentacles in half.

4. Combine calamari in large bowl with the tomatoes, cucumbers, and olives. Add salt and pepper to taste. Toss with the vinaigrette and serve immediately.

TRUFFLED MAC AND CHEESE

JON PRATT

Mac and cheese is a quintessential American delicacy that even in its most basic form has always delivered lots of umami. But Jon Pratt, one of the true American umami pioneers, takes it to dizzying new umami heights with the addition of truffle butter, truffle oil, and wine. The unexpected addition of shallots and garlic adds pleasing and sophisticated flavor dimensions to this easy-to-make dish.

When making the cheese sauce, it is important to add the cheese to the hot cream mixture off the flame to avoid overheating, and to then reheat it very gently. Too much heat will cause the cheese to separate.

Use the best quality ingredients you can find. That certainly goes for the cheeses, but also seek out a good quality imported macaroni. And don't try to get away with store-bought bread crumbs. Take the 15 minutes needed to make your own and savor the difference. If absolutely necessary, use Japanese panko bread crumbs.

SERVES 6

½   pound elbow macaroni

1   tablespoon unsalted butter

1   shallot, minced (about 2 tablespoons)

1   tablespoon minced garlic (approximately 2 large cloves)

½   cup dry white wine

1   quart heavy cream

3   ounces **black truffle** butter (see Sources, page 194)

4½   teaspoons **black truffle** oil

½   pound shredded Italian **fontina cheese**

     Salt and pepper

1   cup Quick Homemade Bread Crumbs (opposite)

¼   cup grated **Parmigiano-Reggiano cheese**

     White truffle oil to drizzle (optional)

1. In a large pot, bring 3 quarts of salted water to a boil. Cook the macaroni al dente. Drain and toss with 1 teaspoon of the unsalted butter to coat. Reserve, covered.

2. Preheat the oven to 400 degrees F.

3. In a medium saucepan set over medium-low heat, sweat the shallots and garlic in the remaining unsalted butter until soft. Avoid getting any color. Add the white wine and reduce until almost dry. Add heavy cream and boil until reduced by half, about 15 minutes.

4. Remove the pan from the heat. Stir in black truffle butter and black truffle oil. Add the fontina and whisk to incorporate. Adjust seasoning with salt and pepper.

5. Add the macaroni to the cheese mixture, return the pan to a burner set to low. Stir gently for 2 minutes to reheat and thicken. Do not boil.

6. Spoon mixture into six 6-ounce ramekins. Top with toasted bread crumbs and grated Parmesan. Bake in oven for 5 minutes until cheese begins to bubble.

7. Drizzle a few drops of white truffle oil on top, if you wish.

QUICK HOMEMADE BREAD CRUMBS

MAKES ABOUT 1 CUP

½   loaf day-old French or Italian bread
2   tablespoons olive oil
     Salt and pepper

1. Preheat the oven to 350 degrees F.

2. Cut bread into ½-inch cubes. Place in a food processor fitted with a metal blade. Pulse 6 or 8 times, until bread is very coarsely chopped. Transfer to a large mixing bowl. Sprinkle with olive oil, season with salt and pepper, and toss gently to coat.

3. Spread the bread crumbs on a cookie sheet and bake for 10 minutes or until golden brown. You may need to stir the bread crumbs halfway through baking so they toast evenly.

4. Transfer the toasted bread crumbs to a cool surface such as another cookie sheet or aluminum foil laid out on the counter.

5. Cool and store in airtight container until needed.

COCONUT–LIME LEAF SOUP

JON PRATT

As chef and co-owner of two Umami Café locations in New York's Hudson Valley, Jon may know more about cooking with umami than any other chef working in America today. And as science now seems to corroborate, Jon has long believed that "the reaction to umami is hard wired in us. It's an animal instinct."

So with nearly four years under his belt cooking with and campaigning for umami among often dubious diners, it is hard to argue when he tells us, "Do not try shortcuts or substitutes!" with his Coconut–Lime Leaf Soup.

In this hybrid of two traditional Thai recipes, tom ka gai and tom yam, basic and synergizing umami come principally from chicken stock and fish sauce. Yet it is really the balance of umami with other tastes and flavors that make this soup so charming and thrilling at the same time. Make the effort to get the ingredients Jon specifies (see Sources, page 194), and follow the directions carefully. It is not difficult, and it is very much worth it.

❝I think the reaction to this stuff is hard wired in us. It's an animal instinct.❞

—JON PRATT

SERVES 8 AS A FIRST COURSE

1	clove garlic, sliced thin
1	tablespoon peanut oil
4½	teaspoons red curry paste
4½	teaspoons massaman curry paste
28	ounces coconut milk (Mae Ploy brand recommended)
2	cups **chicken stock**
¼	cup **fish sauce**
⅓	cup freshly squeezed lime juice
1	stalk lemongrass, white inner core only, smashed and tied in a bundle
2	kaffir lime leaves, torn into small pieces
2	tablespoons plus 1½ teaspoons palm sugar
¼	cup loosely packed Thai basil leaves

FOR GARNISH, YOUR CHOICE OF (ABOUT 1½ CUPS TOTAL)

Cooked diced **chicken**

Cooked diced **shrimp**

Diced **tofu**

Peas

Sliced **shiitake mushrooms**

Cooked rice vermicelli

Sliced scallions

Julienned **carrots**

In a large pot (3 quarts or bigger), sauté the garlic in the oil. Add the curry pastes and stir until soft. Add the chicken stock, fish sauce, lime juice, and 2 cups water, and bring to a simmer. Add lime leaves, lemongrass, and palm sugar and continue to simmer for 10 minutes. Remove the lemongrass and discard. Add the Thai basil and garnishes just before serving.

ANCHOYADE-GRILLED CEDAR-PLANKED BLUEFISH OR SALMON

STEVEN RAICHLEN

According to Steven, "This recipe spans two continents—anchoyade is an anchovy-flavored mayonnaise from Provence in the south of France, while grilling fish on a cedar plank originated with the Native Americans of the Pacific Northwest." Since both of the fish used in this recipe have substantial amounts of both basic and synergizing umami, when you put them together you get a dish that explodes with umami taste. So it is not only delicious by itself, it makes whatever you eat with it taste better, too.

Steven also points out that "the cedar plank adds an interesting wood and spice note of its own and spares you the challenge of turning the fish on the grill (always tricky when grilling delicate fish). If you don't like anchovies—well, you should try this dish anyway—cooking them mellows the flavor. If you absolutely hate anchovies, substitute 3 tablespoons black olive paste."

As you spread the anchoyade onto the fish, you may think there's too much. Do not worry. Follow Steven's instructions. What you want is a generous robe of dressing to surround the fish, which traps the moisture and adds a wonderfully creamy texture.

You will need a cedar plank that is roughly 6 by 14 inches. Use the kind made specifically for grilling, not cedar shingles from a building supply store as they may be chemically treated. According to Steven, cedar grilling planks are available at grill and gourmet shops, or see Sources (page 194) for an online purveyor. To use it, soak the plank in salted water for 1 hour, then drain.

The cedar plank, by the way, makes a unique, rustic tableside presentation. Slice portions right on the wood and serve.

SERVES 4

1	(2-ounce) can **anchovy fillets**, well drained and finely chopped
2	cloves garlic, minced
1	teaspoon finely grated fresh lemon zest
2	tablespoons Dijon mustard
¾	cup mayonnaise (preferably Hellman's)
	Freshly ground black pepper
1½	pounds **bluefish** or **salmon** fillets
	Coarse salt (kosher or sea)

1. To make the anchoyade, place the anchovies, garlic, and lemon zest in a mortar and pound to a smooth paste with a pestle. If you don't have a mortar and pestle, place them in the bottom of a metal mixing bowl and pound with the end of a rolling pin. Add the mustard, mayonnaise, and pepper to taste, and whisk to mix.

2. Set up your grill for indirect grilling (see Note) and preheat to medium-high (400 degrees F). Season the fish on both sides with salt and pepper. (Go easy on the salt—anchovies are salty). Arrange the fish skin side down on the board. Using a spatula, spread the top and sides of the fish with the anchovy mayonnaise.

3. Place the fish on the plank on the grill away from the heat. Close the cover and indirect-grill the fish until the top is darkly browned and bubbling and the fish is cooked through, 20 to 35 minutes. (A metal skewer inserted in the side will come out piping hot to the touch.) Serve the fish right on the plank.

N O T E . For charcoal and wood grills, preparation for indirect grilling means building the fire on one side of the firebox only. On a gas grill, indirect means leaving one or more burners unlit, reserving the grill space over the unlit burners for the food. The food goes over the unlit side on either type of grill.

WOOD-GRILLED RIB STEAK WITH SHIITAKE-WINE SAUCE

STEVEN RAICHLEN

"This recipe is all about meat—from the beefiest of steaks (the rib steak) to the meatiest of mushrooms (shiitakes) to the brawniest of red wines (zinfandel)," Steven tells us. Likewise, it is all about umami, abundant in both basic and synergizing forms in each of the aforementioned. Steven recommends grilling this over the glowing embers of oak logs or wine barrel staves (see Sources, page 194). "At the very least, toss a handful of soaked wine barrel or oak chips on the coals or place in your grill's smoker box."

Steven notes, "A rib steak is a more–than–bible–thick steak with a rib attached. You'll likely need to order it ahead from your butcher or supermarket meat cutter."

SERVES 2 OR 3

1	bone-in **rib steak** (about 2 pounds; 1½- to 2-inches thick)
1	tablespoon extra virgin olive oil
2	cloves garlic, minced
2	tablespoons chopped fresh rosemary, rubbed between your fingers
	Coarse sea salt
	Cracked black peppercorns
	Shiitake-Wine Sauce (opposite)
2	tablespoons finely chopped flat-leaf parsley

1. Lightly brush the steak on both sides with olive oil. Thickly crust each side with garlic and rosemary. Season with salt and pepper. Let the steak marinate in the refrigerator while you build the fire.

2. Set up your grill for direct grilling (which means the grate where the food will be cooked is directly over fire) and make a medium-hot fire. If possible, create a slightly cooler grilling zone to one side.

3. When you are ready to cook, brush and oil the grill grate, and place the steak on top. Grill the steak for 3 minutes, then rotate it a quarter turn to create a handsome crosshatch of grill marks. Continue grilling until the bottom is darkly browned and beads of juice begin to appear on top, 4 to 6 minutes longer.

4.   Turn the steak over and continue grilling until cooked to taste, 7 to 9 minutes, 14 to 18 minutes in all for medium-rare. Again, rotate the steak a quarter turn after 3 minutes of cooking. If the steak starts to brown too quickly, move it to the cooler zone.

5.   Transfer the steak to a platter or cutting board and let it rest for 3 minutes. Cut off the bone and set it aside. If the meat on the bone is too rare, put it back on the grill to crisp.

6.   Thinly slice the steak crosswise. Serve the steak fanned out on plates with the Shiitake-Wine Sauce spooned over it. Sprinkle the parsley over the steak and serve at once.

SHIITAKE-WINE SAUCE MAKES ABOUT 1¼ CUPS

3   tablespoons unsalted butter

3   large shallots, minced (about ¾ cup)

6   ounces **shiitake mushrooms**, stems removed, wiped clean, and thinly sliced

2   cups zinfandel or other full-bodied dry **red wine**

1   cup **beef, veal,** or **chicken stock** (preferably homemade)

1   teaspoon cornstarch (optional)

1   tablespoon syrah **red wine** (optional)

Coarse sea salt and freshly ground black pepper

1.   Melt 2 tablespoons of the butter in a heavy saucepan over medium heat. Add the shallots and cook until soft but not brown, about 3 minutes, stirring often. Add the shiitakes and cook until browned and most of the mushroom liquid has evaporated, about 3 minutes. Add the wine, increase the heat to high, and bring to a boil. Let the wine simmer briskly until reduced by half, about 5 minutes.

2.   Add the stock to the saucepan. Briskly simmer the mixture until reduced to 1 to 1¼ cups, 5 to 10 minutes. If you use very good homemade stock, the mixture may be thick enough to serve as a sauce without adding the cornstarch. If not, dissolve the cornstarch in the syrah and whisk it into the sauce. Let boil until thickened slightly, about 1 minute.

3.   Remove the saucepan from the heat and whisk in the remaining 1 tablespoon butter. Season with salt and pepper to taste; it should be highly seasoned.

PORTOBELLO AND CHANTERELLE MUSHROOM CYLINDER

JIMMY SCHMIDT

Jimmy Schmidt piles on an abundance of basic and synergizing umami, balanced with a taste of sweet from the honey and squash, and a touch of tart from the two wines.

According to Jimmy, "Umami is used to build deep haunting layers of flavors with the mushrooms. The portobello mushrooms also provide a smoky flavor with a silky texture. The chanterelles are sautéed until almost crisp with their own juices concentrated back on them. The truffle oil and Parmigiano support the umami of the chanterelles. The umami of the syrah essence acts as the glue for the salad. These are simple ingredients by themselves but combine to produce more flavor than the parts," which is the very essence of umami synergy.

You will need roasted winter squash for this recipe.

SERVES 2 AS AN APPETIZER

- 2 cups syrah **red wine**
- 2 tablespoons wildflower honey
- Olive oil, for frying
- 2 large sprigs rosemary
- ¼ cup snipped fresh chives
- ¼ cup dry **white wine**
- Sea salt
- Freshly ground Tellicherry black pepper
- 2 medium **portobello mushrooms**
- ¼ pound **golden** and **black chanterelles** of uniform size
- ½ cup diced roasted **winter squash**, warm or room temperature
- 2 cups mâche, cleaned
- 2 tablespoons **white truffle** oil
- 2 tablespoons grated **Parmigiano-Reggiano**

1. Preheat the grill or broiler to high. In a medium nonreactive saucepan, combine red wine and honey. Bring to a simmer over medium-high heat, and cook until thick enough to coat the back of a spoon, about 8 to 10 minutes. Reserve.

2. In a medium skillet, heat about 1 inch of olive oil (at least ¾ cup) over medium heat. When the oil begins to shimmer, but before it starts to smoke, add the rosemary sprigs. Cook until they stop bubbling and are quite crisp, about 4 minutes. Drain the rosemary on paper towels to cool. Reserve the cooking oil. Strip the rosemary leaves from their stems and reserve, discarding the stems.

3. In a blender combine half of the crisp rosemary, half of the chives, the white wine, and a pinch of salt and pepper. Puree until smooth. Slowly add ½ cup of the rosemary-flavored oil and blend until emulsified. Reserve.

4. Remove the gills from the portobello mushrooms and trim the stem even with the cap. Place in a flat pan and coat well with some of the remaining rosemary oil. Season generously with salt and pepper. Place on the grill or under the broiler and cook until softened and well browned, about 6 minutes. Remove and allow to cool.

5. Using the inside of a 3-inch cylinder mold as a guide, cut a perfect round from each portobello. Carefully slice each round horizontally to yield 2 circular mushroom discs per cap. Reserve.

6. In a large nonstick skillet, heat 2 tablespoons of the remaining rosemary oil over high heat; do not allow the oil to smoke. Add the chanterelles, searing very well before agitating in the pan. Season with salt and pepper. Cook about 6 minutes, until the mushroom juices are released and they are concentrated to coat the mushrooms. Transfer to a medium bowl and add the warm winter squash, mâche, half of the red wine essence, and the truffle oil and toss to combine. Sprinkle in the Parmigiano, remaining chives, and half of the remaining crisp rosemary leaves, and toss to combine.

7. Place a cylinder mold in the center of each of two serving plates. Place one portobello disk at the bottom of the mold; you will build on this base. Divide the chanterelle salad between the two molds and press with your fingers to compact. Place the remaining portobello disks on top of each cylinder. Hold down the contents of the cylinder while raising the mold to release. Drizzle the cylinder and plate with the remaining red wine essence and the rosemary-chive–white wine emulsion. Sprinkle with some of the crisp rosemary leaves and a little black pepper. Serve immediately.

VANILLA-SCENTED LOBSTER WITH ASPARAGUS THREAD SALAD

JIMMY SCHMIDT

No culinary wallflower, Jimmy Schmidt goes for bold dishes with immense flavor and big umami, like this clever appetizer salad based on the classic and umami-rich combination of lobster and asparagus. According to Jimmy, "The umami in this recipe is magnified by combining the caramelized asparagus, shiitake mushrooms, and the tender lobster, all splashed with the lemongrass and sake-scented sauce. The flavor theme is layered with vanilla poaching butter, vanilla seeds in the sautéing butter, and vanilla in the vinaigrette for the salad atop the dish. Asparagus is presented as a base and as raw threads in the salad."

SERVES 4 AS AN APPETIZER

2   live **lobsters**, 1½ to 2 pounds each

1   vanilla bean, cut in half the long way, seeds scraped out and reserved

1   cup plus 6 tablespoons (2¾ sticks) unsalted butter, at room temperature

2   tablespoons pure vanilla extract

     Juice and grated rind of 1 large lemon (about ¼ cup juice)

     Sea salt

4   tablespoons extra virgin olive oil

     Freshly ground Tellicherry black pepper

16   large spears **asparagus**, peeled

4   tablespoons snipped fresh chives

1   tablespoon minced shallots

2   teaspoons mild paprika

2   cups dry **sake**

1   cup heavy cream

1   cup **shiitake mushrooms**, stems removed, cleaned

½   cup magenta micro spinach leaves (see Sources, page 194)

TO COOK THE LOBSTERS: In a large pot of boiling water over high heat, cook the lobsters for 6 minutes. Remove and cool to room temperature. Remove tail and claws. Cut tail open and remove meat. Cut tail in half lengthwise. Crack and remove meat from each claw and knuckle. Place in a saucepan just large enough to hold meat. In another small pan, combine the vanilla bean pod and ¾ cup (1½ sticks) of the butter, melt over low heat, and pour over the lobster meat. Reserve off heat.

TO MAKE THE VANILLA BUTTER: Combine the remaining ¼ cup butter, the vanilla bean seeds and scrapings, and 1 tablespoon vanilla extract in a small bowl. Reserve.

TO MAKE THE VANILLA VINAIGRETTE: Combine 2 tablespoons of the lemon juice, the remaining 1 tablespoon vanilla extract, and 2 tablespoons of the olive oil in another small bowl. Season with salt and pepper to taste. Reserve.

TO PREPARE THE ASPARAGUS: Cut asparagus tips to 3 inches in length. Make asparagus thread salad by cutting asparagus stems into long, fine threads with a mandoline or thin sharp knife. Combine asparagus threads with vanilla vinaigrette. Reserve.

TO MAKE THE CHIVE OIL: In a blender, combine remaining lemon juice and olive oil, and half of the chives. Puree until smooth, adding a pinch of salt. Reserve.

TO MAKE THE SAUCE: In a large saucepan, melt 2 tablespoons of the butter over medium-high heat. Add the shallots and cook until translucent, about 4 minutes. Stir in the paprika and cook 1 minute more. Add the sake and cook until reduced to ¼ cup, about 5 minutes. Add the cream and cook until reduced to coat the back of a spoon, about 8 minutes. Strain through a fine sieve into a clean saucepan. Return to a simmer over medium-high heat. Whisk in the remaining 4 tablespoons of butter and the grated lemon rind. Remove from the heat and keep warm, stirring occasionally.

TO COOK THE ASPARAGUS AND SHIITAKES: Divide the vanilla butter between 2 medium nonstick skillets, and heat over medium-high heat. Add the asparagus tips to one pan and the shiitakes to the other pan. Cook until both are caramelized and sweet, about 5 minutes. Season with salt and pepper. Meanwhile, return the lobster in butter to medium heat. Heat slowly until warm. Do not boil.

TO SERVE: Position the asparagus spears with tips toward the top and bottom of the warm serving plates. Position the shiitakes around the asparagus. With a slotted spoon, remove the lobster meat from its butter, drain slightly, and position atop the asparagus tips. Add the micro spinach to the asparagus thread salad, toss to combine, and position atop the lobster. Drizzle the sauce and chive oil over and around the plate. Sprinkle with the remaining chives. Serve immediately.

MY FATHER'S FAMOUS SHRIMP HORS D'OEUVRES

LYDIA SHIRE

"My four children could not fathom Christmas without these!" says Lydia. "My father was a wonderful cook, and I used to help him make these. Now, even my 'fancy' foodie friends can't wait for them."

The umami is concentrated in just two ingredients: shrimp and blue cheese, a powerful, almost unexpected combination of basic and synergizing umami. But they are also pungent, salty, crunchy, and fabulous fun all at the same time. They are really easy to make, and the bread crumbs cover up most cutting and stuffing mistakes, so they look good, too.

Lydia notes that if you cannot find Roka Blue cheese, you can make your own with equal parts of blue cheese and cream cheese. "But, in my opinion, there are times in this world that a little help from a jar actually tastes great. It's the right consistency, and sometimes you must work smarter not harder!"

Wait until the guests arrive to cook these, so they may be served immediately.

SERVES 6

2	pounds cooked, peeled, and deveined **shrimp**, size 16–20 per pound
2	jars Kraft **Roka Blue cheese** (see Note)
2	cups all-purpose flour
2	teaspoons salt
2	teaspoons freshly ground black pepper
3	**eggs**
1	pound panko (Japanese bread crumbs) or 4 cups fresh homemade bread crumbs (page 133)
	Peanut oil, for frying
	Lemon wedges, for garnish
	Parsley, for garnish

1. Find the cut around the outside edge of the shrimp where it was deveined. Use a sharp paring knife to make that cut deeper, almost all the way through to the other side of the shrimp. The end result of doing this properly is that you create a little pocket for filling. Pack in as much Roka cheese as you can; smooth it out so it is flush with the shrimp's sides. Lay completed shrimp on a large plate. Cover with plastic wrap and chill in the refrigerator for 30 minutes.

2. In one bowl, thoroughly combine the flour with the salt and pepper. In another, beat the eggs with 2 tablespoons water. Place the crumbs in a third bowl. Dip each shrimp lightly in flour, shake off the excess. Dip into the egg, making sure the shrimp is totally covered. Finally dip into the crumbs, again making sure it is totally covered. As each shrimp is coated, lay it on a baking sheet, keeping to 1 layer. Cover and return to the refrigerator until ready to cook.

3. Heat 2 to 3 inches of peanut oil in a 4-quart pot to 350 degrees F. (You will know it is ready when a piece of bread dropped in it browns immediately.) The key is to make sure the oil is not so hot that the shrimp browns before the cheese has a chance to melt.

4. Fry 6 shrimp at a time. As they are done, remove from the oil with a slotted spoon. Drain the shrimp on paper towels and serve on a platter garnished with lemon wedges and parsley.

N O T E .   You'll find Roka Blue cheese in little glass jars in or near the dairy section of your supermarket.

LOBSTER AVGOLEMONO

LYDIA SHIRE

"This is probably my second favorite soup in the world," says Lydia, never revealing her first choice. But no matter, this soup stands on its own.

At first, it resembles the classic Greek soup of the same name, but then it doesn't, because Lydia has taken this simple peasant preparation and turned it into something else entirely—something familiar and comforting, yet outlandishly rich, even exotic.

She retains the lemon, of course, as well as the chicken stock and egg yolk essential to the original and both umami loaded. To that she adds lobster, potato, and tomato, which not only build on the umami, but also introduce new dimensions of flavor, texture, acidity, and pure luxury.

The key to success with this soup is never to let it get too hot once the eggs are in. Follow this rule and you will get a thick, creamy, almost custard-like broth. Also, Lydia says, if you do not have homemade broth, use canned. The flavor just won't be quite as rich or deep.

SERVES 6 TO 8

3	Maine **lobsters**, 1 to 1¼ pounds each
2	quarts homemade **chicken stock**
2	ripe **tomatoes**, chopped (optional)
1	large yellow Spanish onion, diced
6	tablespoons (¾ stick) unsalted butter, plus additional for serving
8	small, skin-on **red bliss potatoes**, diced ½-inch
8	**egg yolks**
½	cup freshly squeezed lemon juice
	Salt and freshly ground black pepper
	Chopped garlic chives or regular chives, for garnish

1. Cook the lobsters in rapidly boiling salted water for 5 minutes. Remove and shock in ice water. Take all the meat from claw and tail shells and reserve.

2. In a stockpot or large saucepan, simmer the chicken stock with the lobster bodies. Do not remove the coral or tomalley as they contribute to the flavor of the soup. Add chopped fresh tomatoes (if using). Reduce until you are left with 1 quart of stock. Strain and discard the solids.

3. In separate saucepan, sauté the onion in 4 tablespoons butter until soft. Add the diced potatoes. Pour in the reduced stock and simmer until potatoes are just done al dente, about 15 minutes.

4. Cut the lobster meat into large chunks and sauté in 2 tablespoons butter until heated through, then add to the soup.

5. In a separate bowl, mix the egg yolks with the lemon juice. Ladle 1 cup of the hot liquid slowly into yolk mixture while stirring. Then pour the mixture back into soup. Stir continuously; bring just to the boiling point, but do not boil.

6. Season with salt and pepper. Ladle into bowls, add a small nugget of butter into each. Sprinkle with the chopped chives. Serve immediately.

RED SNAPPER WITH HAM HOCK–RED WINE SAUCE

FRANK STITT

In addition to his superb Provençal-informed interpretations of Southern classics, Frank Stitt likes to surprise. Instead of serving this fish with a traditional light-bodied sauce, he treats it like a cut of red meat with a big, bold sauce of red wines and ham hocks. According to Frank, "This way, you get your healthy piece of fish but also get to enjoy the big flavor of a roast or braised meat." The effect is deeply rich flavors supported by a substantial umami character. This helps keep the flavor of the fish front and center, not drowned out as one might expect.

Frank suggests substituting grouper, halibut, wild striped bass, tuna, swordfish, or salmon. If you wish, make the sauce a day ahead and refrigerate, or freeze it for another time.

SERVES 6

FOR THE SAUCE

1   teaspoon olive oil

1   large yellow onion, diced

1   **carrot**, peeled and sliced

1   stalk celery, sliced

    Bouquet garni of 2 bay leaves, 3 sprigs thyme, 5 sprigs flat-leaf parsley, and 1 dark green leek top (well washed), tied together

2   cups **red wine**

¼   cup **ruby port**

2   smoked **ham hocks**

1   quart homemade **chicken stock** or canned low-sodium **broth**

2   tablespoons unsalted butter

    Salt and freshly ground black pepper

    Red wine vinegar or freshly squeezed lemon juice to taste

FOR THE RED SNAPPER

1   teaspoon olive oil

1   tablespoon unsalted butter

6   (6- to 8-ounce) **red snapper fillets**, skin on

    Kosher salt and freshly ground white pepper

TO MAKE THE SAUCE:

1. Heat the oil in a large pot over medium heat. Add the onion, carrots, and celery and cook until slightly caramelized, about 15 minutes. Add the bouquet garni and deglaze the pot with the red wine and port, stirring up any browned bits. Boil until the wine is reduced by three quarters. Add the ham hocks and chicken stock and bring to a simmer. Simmer very gently for 2½ hours until the meat is quite tender; skim carefully as the stock simmers to remove any fat that rises to the surface.

2. Remove the ham hocks with tongs or a slotted spoon. Strain the stock, return it to a clean pot, and boil over medium-high heat until reduced to 1 cup. Remove from the heat.

3. Meanwhile, when it is cool enough to handle, remove the ham from the bones and tear into small pieces, discarding the fat, skin, and gristle; set aside. (The sauce can be made to this point up to 1 day ahead. Refrigerate the sauce and ham separately.)

4. To finish the sauce, bring it to a simmer and swirl in the butter bit by bit. Add the ham, and season the sauce with salt and pepper and vinegar or lemon juice.

TO MAKE THE RED SNAPPER:

1. In a large, heavy sauté pan, heat the oil and butter over high heat until almost smoking. Season the fish with salt and white pepper and add to the pan skin side down. Lower the heat to medium and cook until the edges just begin to turn opaque, about 4 minutes. Turn over and continue cooking until just opaque throughout, about 4 minutes more. Transfer the fillets to a rack set over a platter and cover to keep warm.

2. Reheat and finish the sauce (if made a day ahead). Place the snapper fillets on dinner plates and spoon the sauce (and ham hocks bits) over and about.

PEA CAKES WITH TOMATO SALSA

FRANK STITT

Frank Stitt turns two staples of the American South, fresh peas and corn bread made with buttermilk and bacon fat, into a wonderfully balanced, basic umami recipe with hints of sweet, sour, and salt from skillful seasoning, as well as a gentle touch of jalapeño heat.

These pea cakes work well with the umami-synergizing effect of grilled meats, or by themselves as hors d'oeuvres.

SERVES 4 AS A SIDE DISH OR APPETIZER

2	cups cooked **Peas** (page 152), such as pink eyes, butter peas (also known as lima beans) or crowders, cooking broth reserved
1	cup crumbled **Corn Bread** (page 152), or more as needed
2	tablespoons chopped chives
1	tablespoon minced hot red chili pepper, such as a ripe jalapeño
1	tablespoon extra virgin olive oil
1	tablespoon all-purpose flour, plus extra for dusting
	Kosher salt and freshly ground black pepper
1	large **egg**, beaten
2	tablespoons vegetable oil
	Tomato Salsa (page 153)

1.   Puree ¾ cup of the peas with ¼ cup of reserved broth in a blender until smooth. Pour into a medium bowl, add the remaining whole peas, 1 tablespoon reserved broth, the corn bread, chives, chili, olive oil, flour, and salt and pepper to taste, and mix well. Add the egg and mix again. You may need to adjust the "wetness" by adding a little more corn bread or broth to the mixture; it should be just moist enough to hold together.

2.   Form 8 to 10 small cakes by shaping portions of the mixture (about 3 table- spoons each) into 2-inch-wide disks, compressing the mixture with your fingers and patting it together.

3.   Heat the vegetable oil in a heavy skillet over medium-high heat. Dust the cakes with a little flour and gently place them, in batches if necessary, in the hot oil. Lower the heat to medium and cook, turning once, until golden brown, about 4 minutes on each side.

4.   Serve hot, topped with Tomato Salsa.

PEAS MAKES ABOUT 2 CUPS PEAS

6	cups water, preferably spring water
1	onion, quartered
1	bay leaf
4	sprigs thyme
4	sprigs savory
	Kosher salt
1	pound shelled small green **butter peas (lima beans)**, picked over and rinsed

Combine the water, onion, bay leaf, thyme, savory, and salt in a medium saucepan and bring to a boil. Reduce the heat to a simmer and cook gently for 15 minutes. Add the beans, adjust the heat to maintain a simmer, and cook until the beans are just tender, 15 to 20 minutes. Taste for seasoning, and add salt if necessary. Remove the pan from the heat and let the beans rest in their liquid for 10 minutes. Drain, reserving the broth but discarding the onion and herbs, and cool.

CORN BREAD MAKES ONE 8- TO 9-INCH LOAF

2	cups self-rising yellow **cornmeal** (or substitute 2 cups regular cornmeal plus 1 teaspoon baking powder, 1 teaspoon baking soda, and ¾ teaspoon salt)
½	cup all-purpose flour
¾	cup whole milk
¾	cup **buttermilk**
	Scant ½ cup rendered **bacon fat** or 7 tablespoons unsalted butter (melted), or scant ½ cup vegetable oil (or a mixture)
1	extra-large **egg**, lightly beaten

1. Preheat the oven to 450 degrees F.

2. Place an 8- to 9-inch cast-iron skillet in the oven.

3. Place the cornmeal and flour in a large bowl and stir in the milk and buttermilk a little at a time, mixing with a large wooden spoon. The batter will be quite loose.

4. Meanwhile, add the bacon fat to the preheated skillet, return it to the oven, and heat until the fat is very hot, about 5 minutes.

5. Remove the skillet from the oven. Pour all but 1 tablespoon of the hot fat into the cornmeal mixture and stir to combine. Add the egg and stir to combine. Pour the batter into the hot skillet and immediately place it in the oven. Bake for 20 to 25 minutes, until golden brown. Remove from the oven and unmold.

TOMATO SALSA

4	firm, ripe Roma **tomatoes**
½	shallot or 2 scallions, finely minced
1	teaspoon **red wine vinegar**
1	teaspoon freshly squeezed lime juice
	Kosher salt
	Freshly ground black pepper
	Small handful fresh cilantro or basil leaves, coarsely chopped
½	teaspoon finely chopped jalapeño pepper
1	tablespoon extra virgin olive oil

Combine all ingredients in a medium mixing bowl. Toss gently to combine. Serve immediately, or keep for 3 to 4 hours at room temperature. Do not refrigerate.

GOAT CHEESE DUMPLINGS WITH MOREL MUSHROOMS

TROY THOMPSON

Early in his cooking career, Troy worked extensively in Japan where he adopted the sensibility of his Japanese colleagues. He believes in an approach that is natural and unforced, one that derives from an intimate understanding of ingredients, not rules or contrivances of fashion. The goat cheese dumplings are puffy little pillows with an agreeable texture and deep flavor from the duo of cheeses. This joins with the sweet, sour, and savory sauce to deliver abundant umami along with stimulating spice notes.

SERVES 8 AS AN APPETIZER OR 4 AS A MAIN COURSE

½   pound soft, fresh **goat cheese**

2   whole **eggs**

2   **egg yolks**

1½ cups grated **Parmesan cheese**

     Pinch of salt

     Pinch of freshly ground black pepper

     Scant pinch of nutmeg

     Scant pinch of cayenne pepper

1   cup all-purpose flour

     Morel Mushroom Sauce (opposite)

     Smoked Paprika Oil (opposite)

1. In an electric mixer with a paddle attachment, mix the goat cheese, eggs, and egg yolks until incorporated and smooth. Add the Parmesan cheese, salt, pepper, nutmeg, and cayenne pepper and mix to blend well. Add the flour and incorporate just until dough comes together. Rest the dough for 15 minutes in the refrigerator.

2. Bring a large pot of salted water to a boil. Use a small ice cream scoop or a tablespoon to make tablespoon-size pillows of dough, dropping them into boiling water. Cook until the dumplings float. Remove with a slotted spoon or skimmer and drain.

3. To serve, arrange the dumplings on individual plates. Divide the Morel Mushroom Sauce on top of the dumplings, and sprinkle the Paprika Oil sparingly around the sauced dumplings on each plate.

MOREL MUSHROOM SAUCE

1	pound fresh **morel mushrooms**, or **shiitakes**, **enokis**, **oysters**, or **eryngi**
½	cup (1 stick) butter
1	shallot, chopped
1	cup **Madeira wine**
1	cup **chicken stock**
1	cup heavy cream
	Salt and freshly ground black pepper
	Finely chopped chives, to garnish
1	small Roma **tomato**, peeled and diced small

1. Clean mushrooms by wiping them with a damp cloth. Trim the tough stem ends. Leave smaller mushrooms intact. Slice larger mushrooms into large bite-size pieces.

2. Melt the butter in a large skillet and sauté the mushrooms and shallot until soft. Deglaze the pan with the Madeira. Bring to a boil and reduce by one half, about 6 minutes. Add the chicken stock. Reduce the liquid by half again, about 10 minutes more. Add ½ cup of the heavy cream. Reduce the sauce by half again, an additional 6 minutes, and add salt and pepper to taste.

3. Whip the remaining ½ cup cream to soft peaks. Fold the whipped cream, chives, and tomato into the sauce. Serve immediately.

SMOKED PAPRIKA OIL MAKES ABOUT ¼ CUP

¼	cup grapeseed oil
1	tablespoon smoked sweet paprika

Combine paprika and oil in a small bottle and shake. Let sit overnight until the paprika settles on the bottom. Pour off the clear oil into a clean bottle.

MISO-SCALLION SONOMA LAMB LOIN

TROY THOMPSON

It looks simple, and true to Troy's philosophy, it is. But it is also packed with an unexpected bounty of flavor and interest, and an amazing measure of umami that heightens the pleasure of anything you serve with it.

In fact, we suggest you keep the accompaniments simple, too—wild rice, simple mashed potatoes, stir-fried or steamed vegetables with a dab of butter—so as to avoid interfering with the pure, concentrated flavor of the succulent lamb.

SERVES 6

½   cup white **miso**

5   stalks of scallions, chopped

¾   cup **sake**

3   cleaned **lamb loins**, 12 to 14 ounces each

2   tablespoons grapeseed oil

    Salt and freshly ground pepper

1. Place the miso and scallions in a bowl and use a whisk to slowly blend in the sake a little at a time, thinning down the miso until it has the consistency of a medium-bodied sauce. Add the lamb loins and turn them to cover completely with the mixture. Cover and refrigerate overnight.

2. Preheat the oven to 400 degrees F.

3. Remove the lamb loins from the marinade and wipe off any excess liquid. Heat the grapeseed oil in a medium ovenproof skillet over medium-high heat and sear the lamb on all sides.

4. Place the skillet in the oven for 5 minutes; turn the lamb once. Take the loins out of the oven and allow them to rest for 5 minutes.

5. Season with salt and pepper to taste, carve across the grain into ½-inch slices, and serve.

66 **The umami is reached when the sensual part of the food is there; the aroma and flavor are sensual. Umami makes the food stand out.** 77

—TROY THOMPSON

BUTTER-POACHED MAINE LOBSTER AND TRUFFLE MASHED POTATO "MARTINI"

RICK TRAMONTO

This has been a signature dish of Rick's for many years: "I love the marriage of lobster and mashed potatoes. To me, it's a tempting juxtaposition of rich man's food meeting poor man's food." It is also a marvelously structured umami combination, bringing together the powerful basic umami of potatoes with loads of synergizing umami in the lobster and two truffle ingredients.

SERVES 6

3   cups warm **Yukon Gold Potato Puree** (opposite)

Chopped **lobster** tail and knuckle meat from Poached Lobster Tails and Claws (page 160)

Juice of ½ orange

1   tablespoon chopped **black truffles**

2   tablespoons **white truffle** oil

Kosher salt and freshly ground black pepper

6   **lobster** claws from Poached Lobster Tails and Claws

1   teaspoon Tramonto's Orange Dust (page 161), for garnish

6   lobster tentacles, for garnish

6   fresh chive spears, for garnish

¼   cup confetti flowers (mixed petals of nasturtiums, geraniums, and violets), for garnish

1.   Gently combine the warm potato puree, warm lobster meat, orange juice, chopped truffles, and truffle oil in a mixing bowl. Season with salt and pepper to taste.

2.   For each serving, put ½ cup of the potato puree mixture in a large, dramatic martini glass. Place a Poached Lobster Claw on top. Garnish with a pinch of Orange Dust, a lobster tentacle, a chive spear, and a sprinkling of confetti flowers.

YUKON GOLD POTATO PUREE

8   Yukon gold or other all-purpose **potatoes** (about 2 pounds), peeled and cut into medium cubes

1   cup heavy cream

½   pound (2 sticks) unsalted butter, cut into small pieces

Kosher salt and freshly ground white pepper

1.   Put the potatoes in a medium saucepan, add enough cold water to cover, and lightly salt the water. Bring to a boil over medium-high heat. Reduce the heat and simmer for about 15 minutes, until just tender. Drain the potatoes.

2.   In a small saucepan, heat the cream and butter over medium heat until the butter melts.

3.   Force the potatoes through a ricer and then press through a tamis or fine-mesh sieve into a bowl. Add the cream and butter mixture and stir until smooth. Season to taste with salt and white pepper. Cover and set aside to keep warm.

POACHED LOBSTER TAILS AND CLAWS

½   cup chopped leeks, white and light green parts only, washed

½   cup chopped onion

½   cup chopped **carrot**

4   sprigs fresh thyme

4   bay leaves

3   live Maine **lobsters**, 1 to 1¼ pounds each

4   cups Beurre Monté (opposite)

1. Put the leeks, onion, carrot, thyme, bay leaves, and 2½ quarts water in a large stockpot. Bring to a boil over medium-high heat. Reduce the heat to a simmer.

2. Meanwhile, kill the lobsters by inserting a sharp knife in the back of the head where it meets the lobster body. This will kill it instantly. Remove the claws (with knuckles still attached) and tails from the lobsters. Reserve 6 tentacles for garnish. Reserve the bodies for another use.

3. Add the claws to the simmering vegetables and water and simmer for 4 minutes. Add the tails and simmer for 4 minutes longer.

4. Drain the claws and tails and immediately submerge in cold water. Drain again.

5. Remove the meat from the claws and tails. Transfer to a bowl and set aside at room temperature to cool. Cover and refrigerate if not continuing directly.

6. Heat the beurre monté over medium heat until barely bubbling. (Don't let the beurre monté get too hot or it will separate.) Add the lobster tail and claw meat so that it is completely submerged, and poach for about 10 minutes, until the lobster is heated through.

BEURRE MONTÉ

1   cup water

2   pounds (8 sticks) unsalted butter, cut into small pieces

In a medium saucepan, bring the water to a boil over medium-high heat. As soon as it starts to boil, remove it from the heat. Slowly whisk in the butter, a few pieces at a time, until all the butter is incorporated.

Transfer to a bowl. Cover to keep warm and set aside until needed.

TRAMONTO'S ORANGE DUST MAKES ABOUT ⅓ CUP

7   oranges

¼   cup sugar

1   teaspoon sea or kosher salt

1. Using a vegetable peeler, remove only the colored part of the orange peel. Cut off any bitter white pith remaining on the peel.

2. Combine the orange peel, sugar, salt, and 2 tablespoons water in a large bowl and mix well. Spread on a baking sheet and set in a warm, dry place for 48 hours, or until completely dried.

3. Transfer to a blender and blend until finely powdered.

4. Strain the powder through a fine-mesh sieve into a small container with a tight-fitting lid. It will keep for 3 to 4 weeks.

PEEKYTOE CRAB SALAD WITH CRISPY SAWAGANI CRAB AND MICROGREENS

RICK TRAMONTO

Rick Tramonto lets crabmeat and soy sauce, both umami staples, speak for them-selves in a beautifully balanced dish of umami, sweet, tart, and salty. Peekytoe crab, harvested on the Maine coast, is a current favorite among many chefs, but any other high quality crabmeat works well. At Tru, this dish is garnished with tiny, fried Sawagani crabs. They are delightful to see and eat, but quite rare, so feel free to eliminate them. Crème fraîche is increasingly easy to find in supermarkets, but sour cream is a popular substitute.

SERVES 6

2 cups Peekytoe or other high quality cooked **crabmeat**, picked over to remove any shell and cartilage

1 cup peeled and finely diced Granny Smith or other tart apple

1 tablespoon grated lemon zest

4 teaspoons freshly squeezed lemon juice

2 tablespoons extra virgin olive oil

 Kosher salt and freshly ground black pepper

1 cup Microgreen Salad (page 164)

3 tablespoons crème fraîche

6 tablespoons **Organic Soy Reduction** (page 164)

1 tablespoon Tramonto's Orange Dust (page 161), for garnish

 Citrus Gelée cubes (page 165), for garnish

¼ cup confetti flowers (mixed petals of nasturtiums, geraniums, and violets), for garnish

6 chive spears, 2½ to 3 inches long, for garnish

6 **Crispy Sawagani Crabs** (page 165), for garnish (optional)

1. Mix the peekytoe crabmeat, apple, lemon zest, lemon juice, and olive oil in a bowl. Season to taste with salt and pepper.

2. For each serving, place a ring mold 2½ inches in diameter and 2 inches high in the center of a plate and fill it with some of the crab salad. Press down on the crab with a spoon to make sure the mold is tightly packed. Gently remove the mold. Alternatively, pile one portion of the crabmeat in the center of the plate.

3. Top the crab with Microgreen Salad. Dot the plate with crème fraîche and drizzle with Organic Soy Reduction. Sprinkle Orange Dust over the dish and garnish with Citrus Gelée cubes and flowers. Place a chive on top of the salad and place a Crispy Sawagani Crab (if using) next to or on top of the salad.

MICROGREEN SALAD MAKES ABOUT 1¼ CUPS

1   cup micro cress or tatsoi (see Sources, page 194)

¼   cup edible flowers, such as nasturtiums, pansies, or roses

1   teaspoon extra virgin olive oil

Kosher salt and freshly ground black pepper

Mix the micro cress and flowers in a small bowl. Toss with the olive oil. Season to taste with salt and pepper. Serve at once.

ORGANIC SOY REDUCTION MAKES ABOUT 1 CUP

5   cups organic **soy sauce**

½   cup honey

1. Put the soy sauce and honey in a saucepan and bring to a simmer over medium-high heat, stirring constantly to dissolve the honey. Reduce to medium and boil for 15 to 20 minutes, or until reduced to about 1 cup.

2. Strain through a fine-mesh sieve into a bowl. Cover with plastic wrap and refrigerate.

CITRUS GELÉE MAKES ABOUT 2 CUPS OF ¼-INCH CUBES

3   cups freshly squeezed orange juice

1   cup **Champagne**

14   sheets gelatin (see Sources, page 194)

1.   In a medium saucepan, bring the orange juice and Champagne to a boil over medium-high heat and cook for 2 to 3 minutes. Remove the pan from the heat and set aside to cool slightly.

2.   Meanwhile, fill a bowl with cool water. Gently drop the gelatin sheets into the water, several at a time, until all are submerged. Let soften and bloom for about 5 minutes.

3.   Using your hands, lift the gelatin sheets from the water and squeeze them gently between your fingers. Transfer the sheets to the orange mixture. Stir gently until dissolved. Strain through a fine-mesh sieve into another bowl.

4.   Pour the mixture into a clean, rimmed 9 by 13-inch baking pan. Chill for 1 hour, or until set. Cut gelée into ¼-inch cubes.

CRISPY SAWAGANI CRABS (OPTIONAL)

2   cups canola oil or olive oil for frying

6   live Sawagani **crabs**

    Kosher salt

In a shallow skillet, heat the oil over medium-high heat until very hot. Using a slotted spoon or tongs, gently lower the crabs into the hot oil. Fry for 1 minute, or until the crabs are bright red, turning once.

Remove with a slotted spoon and drain on paper towels. Sprinkle lightly with salt.

MARINATED SHIITAKE MUSHROOM AND RICE HAND ROLLS

MING TSAI

Ming tells of the time when he apprenticed as a cook in Japan and how the correct preparation of sushi rice was the first essential fundamental he learned. It's not hard to do well, but doing it perfectly, in the manner of a great sushi master, takes great care and considerable practice.

Many people consider rice, even sushi rice, somewhat bland by itself. But as any sushi aficionado will attest, eating rice with umami synergizers, such as shiitake mushrooms, miso, and nori in this case, makes the dish spring to life in your mouth. Of this recipe, Ming says, "If you don't know what's in there, you would swear it's meat, there's so much umami."

Koshihikari is the classic, sticky short-grained rice widely used in sushi and other preparations. Although Japanese in origin, good quality Koshihikari rice is now grown in the United States and is widely available in Asian markets, better-stocked supermarkets, and online (see Sources, page 194).

SERVES 4

½   pound large **shiitake mushroom** caps

½   cup **Miso-Shallot Vinaigrette** (opposite)

     Kosher salt and freshly ground white pepper

8   sheets **nori**

4   cups **Steamed Koshihikari Sushi Rice** (page 168)

1.   In a large bowl, mix the mushrooms with the Miso-Shallot Vinaigrette and marinate for 1 hour.

2.   Preheat the oven to 350 degrees F.

3.   Season the mushrooms with salt and pepper to taste. Place on a cookie sheet or in a roasting pan and roast for 15 minutes. Remove from oven and cool slightly. Cut into ½-inch slices.

4.   Toast the nori sheets over an open flame or in a dry skillet over high heat. They will turn bright green when toasted.

5.   Place a sheet of the nori on a work surface, shiny side down. Spread about ½ cup of the rice onto the lower half of the nori, patting it down lightly. Top with a small amount of roasted mushrooms, arranging them diagonally across the rice from the upper left to bottom right. Fold the lower left-hand corner of the nori toward the right side to enclose the filling. Continue to roll toward the nori's right side to form a cone. Repeat with the remaining nori, rice, and mushrooms. Serve immediately.

MISO-SHALLOT VINAIGRETTE MAKES ABOUT 1½ CUPS

¼   cup **shiro miso**

¼   cup sliced shallots

¼   teaspoon shichimi togarashi (Japanese seven-spice powder), or chili pepper

¾   teaspoon sugar

Juice of ½ lemon

2   tablespoons naturally brewed **rice wine vinegar**

¼   teaspoon sesame oil

¾   cup grapeseed or canola oil

Kosher salt and freshly ground black pepper

In a blender, combine the miso, shallots, togarashi, sugar, lemon juice, vinegar, and sesame oil, and blend at high speed until smooth. Drizzle the grapeseed oil slowly into the blender to emulsify. Season with salt and pepper to taste. Store in a covered glass jar in the refrigerator for up to 2 weeks.

STEAMED KOSHIHIKARI SUSHI RICE

There are as many techniques for making sushi rice as there are sushi makers, but here is a reliable method for making the 4 cups of cooked Koshihikari rice called for in Ming's recipe. But remember: Rice, cooking pots, and cooking temperatures can vary, so if you don't like the results the first time you make this, make adjustments the next time.

1½ cups Koshihikari **rice**
2   cups spring water

1.   Place the rice in a large bowl. Add cold water to cover. Swish the rice around in the water with your fingers to rinse off starch. Drain the water and repeat the process until the rinsing water runs clear.

2.   Transfer the rice to a medium pot with a tight-fitting lid. Add the spring water and cover the pan. Bring just to a boil, then immediately reduce the heat to a slow simmer. Cook until the rice has absorbed all the water, 25 to 30 minutes. Do not stir the rice during cooking.

3.   When all the water is absorbed (to check, poke the handle of a fork into the center of the rice in the pan and look for liquid), remove the pan from the heat, leave the lid on, and let the rice rest for 20 minutes with the cover on, to let the moisture equalize in the rice. Remove the cover, fluff lightly with a fork and spread out on a parchment-lined sheet pan to cool.

ꞌꞌ Umami makes food linger on the palate. ꞌꞌ
—MING TSAI

UNI BISQUE

MING TSAI

Uni is the roe of a sea urchin, a spiny-shelled marine animal and a cousin of the starfish. It has long been prized by Japanese cooks for its rich flavor and powerful umami kick. Ming himself reports that uni is one of his favorite ingredients.

Each sea urchin produces five sections of roe, called tongues, that somewhat resemble the sections of an orange. Once rarely seen in U.S. markets (most of the U.S. harvest was sent to Japan), uni is catching on with both chefs and home cooks. Ask your fishmonger to get some for you, or order online (see Sources, page 194). For its distinctive flavor and substantial umami content—fortified in this soup with sake and dashi broth—finding the ingredients and making this soup is well worth the effort required.

Ming suggests serving this soup simply, perhaps in a small rice bowl, or if uni is in season and you buy whole sea urchins, you might wash out the shells and serve it in those. This is such an intensely flavored soup, servings are small—about one cup per person.

SERVES 2

	Peanut oil
6	shallots, peeled and sliced
1	teaspoon minced ginger
	Kosher salt and freshly ground white pepper
½	cup **sake**
4	cups **Dashi** (page 15), or **fish stock**
5	large **sea urchin tongues**, picked over for debris
3	tablespoons cold butter, cut into small pieces
	Chopped chives, for garnish

In a saucepan over medium-high heat, add a small amount of oil and then the shallots and ginger. Season with salt and pepper. Sauté until softened and fragrant, about 1½ to 2 minutes. Deglaze the pan with the sake and reduce until almost dry. Add the dashi and reduce by half, about 20 minutes. Reduce to simmer and add the uni tongues and butter. Transfer to a blender and puree until smooth, or use a hand blender directly in the cooking pot. Taste and correct seasonings. Serve garnished with chopped chives.

SHRIMP UGGIE

ANTHONY UGLESICH

This book is being written on a cusp of American culinary history. It's a time when we mourn the imminent closing of Uglesich's, a shrine to New Orleans seafood. But it's too soon to know if Anthony with his wife and partner Gail, have resurfaced—in either the same or a new incarnation—by the time this book is in print. And while they deserve respite from a lifetime of toils at the stove, we can all hope, selfishly, that they are back.

But gone or not, what remains are the lessons the Uglesichs taught on the importance of absolute freshness, uncompromising quality, and unpretentious food that just plain tastes great. Like Shrimp Uggie.

This recipe was named after Anthony and Gail's son John, who earned the nickname Uggie in grade school when his classmates found it hard to pronounce his last name. It has umami from the ketchup, shrimp, and potatoes, an ingenious concoction that works extremely well. The umami is there not because Anthony thought about it, but as is the case with so many good cooks, it is there because these ingredients taste good together, and Anthony just knows it.

If you can find fresh, locally caught shrimp, the kind the Uglesichs insist on, by all means use them. If not, buy the very best shrimp you can find. This is a simple dish that relies on fresh flavors.

The sauce recipe makes enough for 10 to 12 servings; keep what you don't use covered in the refrigerator, and use within 30 days .

SERVES 2

FOR THE SAUCE

3   cups vegetable oil

1   cup **ketchup**

5   tablespoons (½ bottle) Melinda Extra Hot Sauce

2   tablespoons freshly squeezed lemon juice

2   tablespoons salt

2   teaspoons paprika

4   teaspoons crushed red pepper flakes

1   small red onion, coarsely chopped

1   green bell pepper, coarsely chopped

FOR THE POTATOES AND SHRIMP

2   small-to-medium red or Yukon gold **potatoes**

8 to 10 medium **shrimp**, peeled and deveined with tails left on

2   teaspoons finely chopped fresh parsley

1. Mix the oil, ketchup, hot sauce, lemon juice, salt, paprika, pepper flakes, onion, and bell pepper in a container and let marinate in the refrigerator for 1 day.

2. Place the potatoes in a small pot and cover with cold water. Bring to a boil over medium-high heat. Boil the potatoes 10 to 20 minutes, depending on size, until just cooked through (check by spearing with a paring knife). Cut into 1-inch cubes.

3. Place a medium skillet on the stove over medium heat.

4. Remove the sauce from the refrigerator and stir well with a ladle, making sure to bring the solids up from the bottom. Pour enough marinade into the skillet to partly cover the shrimp. Add the shrimp and potatoes. Cook, stirring constantly and turning until the shrimp turn pink, about 5 minutes.

Pour shrimp, potatoes, and all the sauce on two plates and sprinkle with the parsley.

N O T E . Leave the tail on the shrimp, it helps prevent shrinkage. It will take longer to cook a larger shrimp than a smaller shrimp. These are plain boiled potatoes, not seasoned. French bread is good to dip into the sauce

OYSTER SHOOTERS À LA UGLESICH

ANTHONY UGLESICH

Anthony Uglesich always bought oysters from P&J Oyster Company in the New Orleans French Quarter. And while you could do the same (see Sources, page 194), you can still adhere to Anthony's philosophy by tirelessly searching far and wide for the best damn oysters you can find, preferably from waters close to home. Oysters, of course, are loaded with basic and synergizing umami, and they are the undisputed star of this brilliantly simple dish. The balsamic vinegar and sun-dried tomatoes add a little extra umami kick. They also contribute acid as well as sweetness (along with the cane syrup), for a perfect, gratifying balance of tastes.

SERVES 6

2   cups olive oil (not extra virgin)

½   cup **balsamic vinegar**

¼   cup Steen's Cane Syrup (see Sources, page 194)

1   teaspoon salt

1   teaspoon freshly ground black pepper

1   teaspoon cayenne pepper

½   teaspoon dried basil

½   teaspoon dried thyme

½   teaspoon dried oregano

2   tablespoons minced **sun-dried tomatoes**
     (dried, not packed in oil)

24   large **oysters**
     Romaine lettuce leaves, for serving

1. In a covered quart container, mix the oil, vinegar, syrup, salt, peppers, basil, thyme, oregano, and tomatoes. Let the marinade sit—the longer it sits, the better it gets.

2. Shuck the oysters, reserving the liquor and shells.

3. In a medium nonreactive skillet, cook the oysters over medium heat in four batches with their liquor and about ½ cup of the marinade for each batch, just until they start to curl. Do not overcook!

4. Place each oyster back in a shell. Drizzle a little bit of the hot marinade from the pan onto each oyster. Keep warm until all batches are done.

5. Serve 4 oysters per person on the half-shell, on a bed of romaine lettuce.

DEEP-FRIED SUSHI WITH WASABI MISO

NORMAN VAN AKEN

The umami formula is a simple combination of tuna, soy sauce, fish sauce, and miso. But the effect is more than sufficient, because in this case, umami is no more (and certainly no less) than a savory base for a range of other tastes and fabulous flavors and textures in Norman's smart integration of two Pacific classics: Japanese sushi and Filipino lumpia.

SERVES 4

1½	cups various vegetables (carrots, celery, seeded zucchini and yellow squash) cut into matchsticks about 2 inches long
1	tablespoon canola or peanut oil
½	cup **Ginger-Soy Vinaigrette** (opposite)
	Kosher salt
	Freshly cracked black pepper
4	Lumpia Wrappers (page 177)
4	strips sushi-grade **tuna**, or other highest quality sushi fish (5 x ½ x ½-inch each)
	Peanut or canola oil, for frying the lumpias
	Wasabi Miso (page 176)

1. Sauté the vegetables in the canola oil in a very hot wok or sauté pan. When they are cooked al dente, add enough of the vinaigrette to just coat them and remove from heat. Cool in a strainer to allow all of the excess liquid to drain off. Season with salt and pepper to taste.

2. Lay out lumpia wrappers one at a time. Center the vegetables and a strip of the fish on the lower third of each wrapper. Roll up until almost closed, folding in the sides as you do. Seal with water by rubbing the lumpia's edge with your moistened finger and roll completely closed.

3. Pour peanut oil into a skillet to a depth of about 1 inch. Heat over medium-high heat until it reaches 350 degrees F. Carefully add the filled lumpias and fry, turning if necessary, until crispy and golden brown on all sides, about 5 minutes. Remove with tongs and drain on paper towels. Trim ends and slice lumpia into 1-inch disks. Serve immediately, with dipping sauce on the side.

GINGER-SOY VINAIGRETTE MAKES ABOUT 3½ CUPS

1	cup **red wine vinegar**
½	cup **soy sauce**
½	cup dark roasted sesame oil
½	cup olive oil
½	cup chopped cilantro leaves
3	tablespoons minced ginger
3	tablespoons minced garlic
4½	teaspoons sugar
	Freshly cracked black pepper

In a 1-quart jar with a screw-top, combine the vinegar, soy sauce, sesame and olive oils, cilantro, ginger, garlic, and sugar. Shake well, and season to taste with pepper. Keep at room temperature if using immediately. Otherwise refrigerate until needed. Shake well before using. Store unused portion covered in the refrigerator for up to 7 days.

WASABI MISO MAKES ABOUT ½ CUP

2	tablespoons minced ginger
½	teaspoon lightly chopped garlic
1	tablespoon **fish sauce**
1½	teaspoons sugar
	Juice of ½ lime
¼	jalapeño pepper, stem and seeds discarded, minced
	Large pinch of freshly ground black pepper
1½	teaspoons grated lemon zest
1	teaspoon black sesame seeds
¼	Scotch Bonnet pepper, stem and seeds discarded, minced
2	tablespoons dark roasted sesame oil
3	tablespoons extra virgin olive oil
2	teaspoons unsalted organic white **miso**
	Dash of Pick-a-Peppa Sauce
1½	teaspoons Wasabi Paste (below)
	Freshly cracked black pepper

Pulse the ginger, garlic, fish sauce, sugar, lime juice, jalapeño, and ground black pepper with 2 tablespoons water in a food processor. Allow to infuse at least 3 hours, then strain through a fine-mesh strainer back into the blender. Add the lemon zest, sesame seeds, Scotch bonnet, sesame and olive oils, miso, Pick-a-Peppa sauce, and Wasabi Paste and blend until emulsified. Season with cracked pepper to taste. Chill and reserve until needed.

WASABI PASTE MAKES ABOUT ½ CUP

½	cup wasabi powder
1	teaspoon honey
	Juice from ½ lime

In a small bowl, stir together the wasabi powder with water, a little at a time, until it becomes a smooth paste. Stir in the honey and lime juice. Reserve. Store unused portion covered in the refrigerator for up to 30 days.

LUMPIA WRAPPERS

You can find these pre-made at Filipino grocers or online (see Sources, page 194). But they are simple enough to make yourself.

MAKES ABOUT 6 WRAPPERS

1   cup all-purpose flour
    Pinch of kosher salt
1   **egg**, slightly beaten

1. Put the flour and salt in a medium bowl. Add the egg and 1 cup water and whisk until smooth. The consistency should be like thin pancake batter. Rest the batter for 5 minutes before proceeding.

2. Heat a 10-inch nonstick skillet over medium heat. Pour about 3 fluid ounces of batter into the skillet and immediately swirl the batter around to cover the bottom of the pan. When the edges turn golden and lift slightly from the pan, about 2 minutes, turn the wrapper over and cook the other side, about 1 minute more.

3. Repeat until all the batter is used up.

PAN-ROASTED CUMIN-RUBBED BREAST OF CHICKEN WITH PLANTAIN–FOIE GRAS "MOFONGO" ON MY *VERY* BLACK BEAN SAUCE

NORMAN VAN AKEN

*Norman shot to fame by reimagining traditional foods of the New World, specifi-
cally, the Caribbean, Cuba, and South Florida, and fearlessly reaching across oceans
and continents to find ingredients and techniques to bring his ideas to the table. This is a
fine example, and shows us once again that umami knows no borders.*

SERVES 4 FOR DINNER

4	boneless **chicken breasts**, skin intact
	Mofongo (opposite)
	Calypso Spice Rub (page 180)
¼	cup **cornmeal**
¼	cup flour
	Salt and freshly ground pepper
2	tablespoons peanut oil
2	cups **My *Very* Black Bean Sauce** (page 181)

1. Preheat the oven to 400 degrees F.

2. Cut a pocket in the underside of each chicken breast. Stuff with the Mofongo. Cover the pockets back up and season each stuffed breast with the Calypso Rub.

3. Combine the flour and cornmeal with salt and pepper to taste and dredge the breasts. Set aside.

4. Heat the peanut oil in a large, heavy skillet over high heat. Begin cooking the breasts skin side down. Allow to get crisp on the first side, about 2 minutes. Turn the breasts over and let them get crisp on the other side. Place the skillet in the oven and cook about 10 minutes. Remove from the oven and allow to rest.

5. Return the *Very* Black Bean Sauce to high heat and season with about ¼ teaspoon of the Calypso Rub, or to taste.

6. Place about ½ cup of the bean sauce onto the bottom of four warm attractive plates. Center the cooked, stuffed chicken on top of the beans. Serve.

MOFONGO

¼   cup peanut oil

1   very ripe plantain, peeled and sliced ½-inch thick

2   ounces foie gras, cut into very small pieces (optional)

4   tablespoons (½ stick) unsalted butter, cut into
     very small pieces, at room temperature

Salt and freshly ground black pepper

Heat a sauté pan over high heat until quite hot. Add the peanut oil and fry the plantain pieces until quite dark on all sides. Remove them to paper towels to drain. Place the cooked plantain in a bowl and mash in the foie gras (if using) and the butter. Season with salt and pepper to taste.

CALYPSO SPICE RUB MAKES APPROXIMATELY 1½ CUPS

4	tablespoons cumin seeds
2	tablespoons coriander seeds
2	tablespoons yellow mustard seeds
2	tablespoons whole cloves
4	tablespoons whole black peppercorns
2	tablespoons powdered ginger
2	tablespoons ground cinnamon
4	tablespoons dark brown sugar
2	tablespoons ground ancho chili
1	tablespoon kosher salt

Toast the cumin, coriander, mustard seeds, cloves, and black peppercorns in a dry skillet over medium heat until fragrant, 1 to 2 minutes. Cool and grind together in a spice grinder or blender, or with a mortar and pestle. Mix with the ginger, cinnamon, sugar, ancho chili, and salt. Store in a tightly closed jar. Keeps indefinitely.

MY *VERY* BLACK BEAN SAUCE

1	ounce smoked **bacon**, diced small (about ¼ cup)
1½	teaspoons pure olive oil
1	tablespoon unsalted butter
3	cloves garlic, chopped fine
2	small jalapeño peppers, stems and seeds discarded, minced
½	medium red onion, peeled and diced small
1	large stalk celery, cleaned and diced small
1	small **carrot**, peeled and diced small
1½	teaspoons cumin seeds, toasted and ground
1½	teaspoons black peppercorns, toasted and ground
1	bay leaf, broken
¼	cup Spanish **sherry vinegar**
1	cup dried **black beans**, rinsed, soaked in water overnight, and drained
2	**ham hocks**
5	cups **chicken stock**
	Freshly ground black pepper
	Salt
	Pinch of Calypso Spice Rub

1. Heat a saucepan over medium heat. Add in the bacon and olive oil. Allow the bacon to cook until almost done. Add the butter. When the butter foams, add the garlic and jalapeños. Allow them to flavor the fats first, stirring (only about 30 seconds). Turn the heat to medium-high and add the onion, celery, and carrot. Stir to coat. Cook until some nice carmelization occurs, stirring occasionally, about 10 minutes. When the vegetables are nicely caramelized add the cumin, black pepper, bay leaves, vinegar, drained beans, ham hocks, and chicken stock and bring to a boil. Skim off any impurities that come to the surface with a spoon.

2. Reduce the heat to medium-low and cook the beans, uncovered, until they are just soft, 1½ to 2 hours. Add more stock or water as necessary. Season with salt and pepper and a pinch of Calypso Spice Rub to taste.

YUBA WON TONS WITH KUROBUTA AND MATSUTAKE BROTH

ALAN WONG

Alan amasses basic and synergizing umami in this dish with a combination of pork, chicken, and shrimp, topped off with richly flavored mushroom and a touch of yuba, the skin of soy bean curd. Balancing flavors emphasize the pungency of garlic, scallion, and chives, giving the dish an especially vivid quality.

Kurobuta pork comes from the Berkshire or black hog, one of the heritage breeds of pig now enjoying revivals among independent producers in the United States and abroad. Richly marbled, with a deep, satisfying flavor, this is not the "other white meat" that Americans in particular find in the typical supermarket. Kurobuta pork is widely available online (see Sources, page 194) and from many high-end butchers.

Matsutakes are the cherished "pine mushroom" of Japan where they are called the king of mushrooms. They are produced elsewhere in the world, including the American Pacific Northwest. With their intense cinnamon spice aroma, there is nothing else like them. If you can't get them and still want to make this recipe, you might consider something reckless like substituting shiitakes or morels.

SERVES 4 AS A FIRST COURSE

1	pound **ground Kurobuta pork**
1	tablespoon minced garlic
½	cup thinly sliced scallions
1	tablespoon sesame oil
	Salt and freshly ground black pepper
1	quart **chicken stock**
¼	pound **matsutake mushrooms**, wiped clean and sliced lengthwise at least ¼-inch thick
8	medium **shrimp** (21–25 per pound size), peeled and deveined
1	sheet **yuba**, cut into 4 pieces (see Sources, page 194)
	Chopped chives or scallions, for garnish

1. Combine the pork, garlic, sliced scallions, and sesame oil. Season with salt and pepper to taste. Divide and roll into sixteen 1-ounce balls.

2. Bring chicken stock to a boil. Add pork balls. Turn down to a simmer. Add matsutake and let simmer for 5 minutes. Add shrimp and yuba. Season with salt and pepper. Let simmer until pork balls and shrimp are cooked through, 3 to 4 minutes more. Serve in bowls garnished with chopped chives or scallions.

❝ I often tell the cooks to use umami ingredients in their creations, as they will make them taste better. The incorporation of a certain umami ingredient can add a spark to a dish or give it depth or character. It's like a sixth sense, an added skill or taste to acquire. **❞**

—ALAN WONG

FRESH UNI IN FLAVORED TOMATO WATER

ALAN WONG

This is a direct, uncomplicated recipe that emphasizes clean, fresh, distinct flavors and a big umami blast from the olives, tomato, and uni (sea urchin roe).

Yet, despite its simplicity, it is also a study in balance. Alan touches on every taste. He layers on herbal and vegetal notes, and engages the mouth and nasal passages with a wallop of wasabi. There is a full range of textures—from the liquid broth, to the creamy uni, to the crunch of scallions and fennel, and everything in between.

It's also great fun to eat.

SERVES 4 AS AN APPETIZER

1	tablespoon wasabi powder
4	niçoise **olives**, pitted
16	scallion slivers (from 1 scallion, sliced on the diagonal)
8	paper-thin slices fennel bulb
4	shiso leaves, thinly sliced
4	fresh basil leaves, thinly sliced
4	**ume plums**, minced
½	**tomato**, seeded and diced into 16 pieces
4	**uni tongues** (see page 169)
½	cup **Tomato Water** (opposite)
4	sprigs chervil

1.   Mix the wasabi with ½ teaspoon water in a small bowl to form a thick paste. Form 4 pearl-sized balls from the paste.

2.   Take 4 sake cups and add to each cup in the following order: 1 olive, 2 scallion slivers, 2 fennel slices, 1 sliced shiso leaf, 1 sliced basil leaf, some of the ume plum, 4 tomato pieces, 2 more scallion slivers, 1 uni tongue, 1 wasabi pearl, 2 tablespoons of Tomato Water, and a chervil sprig. Consume the contents of the cup in one gulp.

TOMATO WATER   MAKES 2¼ CUPS

5   large **tomatoes**, coarsely chopped
4½ teaspoons salt

1.   In a blender, combine the tomatoes and salt, and blend until smooth. Pour into a strainer with a disposable coffee filter or cheesecloth placed over a bowl. Refrigerate to drain overnight; do not press.

2.   Remove the filter paper and reserve the pulp for another use. Keep the strained liquid refrigerated until serving time.

DIRECTORY OF FEATURED CHEFS

JODY ADAMS

RIALTO, CAMBRIDGE; BLU, BOSTON
WWW.RIALTO-RESTAURANT.COM

Like many accomplished chefs, Jody Adams's appreciation for food and cooking goes back to her childhood and her mother, an adventurous cook herself. After graduating in anthropology from Brown University, she took a part-time job with food writer and teacher Nancy Verde Barr, which refocused her energy and awakened her true passion. Her professional cooking career began as a line cook under chef Lydia Shire. But it was her work at Michelas that drew attention and a following. Within four months of opening Rialto in 1994 with Michela Larson and Karen Haskell, she received praise for her imaginative food that combines New England ingredients and Italian culinary traditions. *Bon Appétit* called Rialto one of the top hotel restaurants in the country.

RICK BAYLESS

TOPOLOBAMPO AND FRONTERA GRILL, CHICAGO
WWW.FRONTERAKITCHENS.COM/RESTAURANTS

Rick Bayless's family was known for their barbecue restaurants in Oklahoma City, but his passions took him to Mexico. His restaurants—Frontera Grill, which specializes in contemporary regional cooking, and Topolobampo, called one of America's only fine-dining Mexican restaurants—have received numerous kudos and awards. The *International Herald Tribune*'s Patricia Wells called Frontera Grill the third best casual restaurant in the entire world. He also has his own line of prepared foods under the Frontera Foods brand.

DANIEL BOULUD

DANIEL, CAFÉ BOULUD, AND DB BISTRO MODERNE, NEW YORK;
CAFÉ BOULUD, PALM BEACH
WWW.DANIELNYC.COM

Born in France and raised on the family farm, Daniel Boulud trained in his native country under some of France's most respected chefs. Since opening Daniel in 1993, he has been honored with four stars from the *New York Times* as well as being rated one of the ten best in the world by the *International Herald Tribune*. His professional achievements and industry awards—from the James Beard Foundation to the Mobil Travel Guide—are legendary and far too numerous to mention.

GARY DANKO

RESTAURANT GARY DANKO, SAN FRANCISCO
WWW.GARYDANKO.COM

Gary Danko is a Culinary Institute of America graduate, yet he first learned to cook at his mother's knee, where he was taught the importance of fresh ingredients and simple seasonings. Today, he is known for using classical training to interpret culinary traditions from around the world. For three consecutive years his restaurant was selected as a Relais & Chateaux property. Last year he received a second consecutive AAA Five-Diamond award, and captured a sixth Five-Star rating from Mobil.

HUBERT KELLER

FLEUR DE LYS, SAN FRANCISCO
WWW.FLEURDELYSSF.COM

Born in France into a family of pastry chefs, Hubert Keller trained under culinary giants Paul Bocuse, Gaston Lenotre, and Roger Vergé, for whom Hubert managed the La Cuisine du Soleil restaurant in San Paulo. Nineteen years ago he become the co-owner of Fleur de Lys, and his traditional French cooking with a Mediterranean accent has been praised by the country's top food critics for unerring quality and healthful ingredients and techniques. Among his numerous awards are the James Beard Foundation Award for American Express Best Chef California, "Top 25 Restaurants in America" from *Food & Wine*, and the DiRoNa Award from *Nation's Restaurant News*.

CHRISTOPHER KIMBALL

FOUNDER AND PUBLISHER, *COOK'S ILLUSTRATED* AND *COOK'S COUNTRY* MAGAZINES; COOKBOOK AUTHOR AND HOST OF *AMERICA'S TEST KITCHEN* ON PBS TELEVISION
WWW.COOKSILLUSTRATED.COM

Christopher Kimball's connection to the kitchen and food goes back to summers as a young boy in the Vermont farmhouse kitchen of friend and baker Marie Briggs, where he spent much time watching her cook. Today, he is considered one of the world's top experts in recipe and kitchen tool testing. He and his professional staff have spent tens of thousands of hours testing and retesting all kinds of recipes and equipment. Their conclusions are published in his two magazines and dozens of highly regarded books.

JAKE KLEIN

PULSE, NEW YORK

WWW.MYRIADRESTAURANTGROUP.COM/PULSE/

Food has always been in Jake Klein's life. His grandfather owned Miami's legendary Raphil's, his mother was that city's premier restaurant publicist, and his stepfather is the award-winning Steven Raichlen. Klein began his career at Pacific Time in Miami, and later became head chef of a catering company whose customers included Martha Stewart and Billy Joel. He then went to cook in Hong Kong, where he laid the foundation for his Asian sensibilities and Asian/Pacific Rim style. He was described by *Esquire* as "a rising star and one of the chefs to watch for in the coming millennium."

NOBUYUKI MATSUHISA

NOBU, NEW YORK, MALIBU, TOKYO, MILAN, MIAMI, LONDON, LOS ANGELES, LAS VEGAS; MATSUHISA, BEVERLY HILLS, ASPEN

WWW.NOBUMATSUHISA.COM

Nobu got his start working in sushi bars in his homeland of Japan. He then worked in Peru, Buenos Aires, Alaska, and Los Angeles, where he opened his first restaurant, the widely praised Matsuhisa, eighteen years ago. A year later he partnered with actor Robert DeNiro to open Nobu in New York, which was awarded Best New Restaurant by the James Beard Foundation. He and his partners operate eight more Nobu establishments around the world.

MARY SUE MILLIKEN AND SUSAN FENIGER

BORDER GRILL, SANTA MONICA AND LAS VEGAS; CIUDAD, LOS ANGELES

WWW.BORDERGRILL.COM; WW.CIUDAD-LA.COM; WWW.MARYSUEANDSUSAN.COM

Mary Sue Milliken and Susan Feniger are hands-on owner-operators of the ever-popular and critically acclaimed Border Grill and Ciudad restaurants. They've appeared in nearly 400 episodes of the Food Network's *Too Hot Tamales* and *Tamales World Tour*, and host a morning food-talk show on KFI 640AM, Los Angeles. They also created Border Girls brand fresh prepared foods for Whole Food Markets, as well as a line of signature pepper mills. Called trailblazers for turning street food and comfort food into critically-acclaimed cuisine, they are both classically trained: Feniger graduated from the Culinary Institute of America and Milliken from Washburne in Chicago.

PATRICK O'CONNELL

THE INN AT LITTLE WASHINGTON, LITTLE WASHINGTON, VIRGINIA
WWW.THEINNATLITTLEWASHINGTON.COM

A self-taught chef, Patrick O'Connell has been called "the Pope of American Haute Cuisine." The Inn at Little Washington was selected as one of the top ten restaurants in the world by the *International Herald Tribune* and is consistently rated number one in all categories by the Washington, DC Zagat Restaurant Survey. What began as a little restaurant in a former garage has won nearly every culinary plaudit of note.

BRADLEY OGDEN

LARK CREEK INN, LARKSPUR, CALIFORNIA; BRADLEY OGDEN, LAS VEGAS
WWW.LARKCREEK.COM

When Bradley Ogden graduated with honors from the Culinary Institute of America, he also received the Richard T. Keating Award for the student Most Likely to Succeed. In 2000, the CIA honored him with the Chef of the Year award. Today, he and his wife Jody co-own eight successful restaurants with Michael and Leslye Dellar. He received the 2004 Illy Best New Restaurant Award from the James Beard Foundation for his eponymous restaurant in Las Vegas; has been called the "Best of the Best" by the *Robb Report*; and honored as among "America's Best Restaurants" by *Gourmet*. His enduring success can be attributed to bringing farm-fresh foods and an innovative culinary flair to his dishes.

KEN ORINGER

CLIO, BOSTON
WWW.CLIORESTAURANT.COM

Ken Oringer got a taste of the restaurant business at 16 when he was a dish washer in a New Jersey restaurant. He first pursued studies in hotel management, and then went on to the Culinary Institute of America where he was voted Most Likely to Succeed. As executive chef and co-owner of the landmark Clio restaurant in Boston, he pushes the boundaries of originality and inspiration in his Asian-inspired dishes. Nominated twice for Best Chef in the Northeast by the James Beard Foundation, he won in 2001. He has been praised by publications such as the *New York Times*, *Food & Wine*, and *Travel & Leisure*, to name a few.

MARK PEEL

CAMPANILE, LOS ANGELES
WWW.CAMPANILERESTAURANT.COM

Once a fry cook at a 24-hour freeway truck stop, celebrated chef Mark Peel first met his mentor, Wolfgang Puck, when he took a job prepping vegetables at Ma Maison in L.A. As part of Ma Maison's informal apprenticeship program, he was sent to work at two French three-star restaurants, La Tour d'Argent and Moulin de Mougins. He worked at the renowned Alice Waters's Chez Panisse, and as head chef at Spago under Puck again. Peel has been honored several times by the James Beard Foundation, and received awards from *Food & Wine* magazine, *Nation's Restaurant News*, and DiRoNA.

JON PRATT

UMAMI CAFÉ, CROTON-ON-HUDSON AND FISHKILL, NEW YORK; PETER PRATT'S INN, YORK-TOWN HEIGHTS, NEW YORK
WWW.UMAMICAFE.COM; WWW.PRATTSINN.COM

An early and earnest pioneer of umami in America, Jon Pratt has won accolades from the *New York Times*, Zagat—"creative, eclectic, wonderful", *Esquire*, and *Wine Spectator* for his imaginative, palate-awakening creations drawing on myriad global cuisines. All are focussed on maximizing the umami experience for his guests. His motto, "Think globally, eat locally."

STEVEN RAICHLEN

AUTHOR, TELEVISION HOST, AND COOKING TEACHER
WWW.BARBECUEBIBLE.COM

Steven Raichlen is a multi award—winning author, journalist, cooking teacher, and television host. His recipes and PBS television show have been credited with reinventing American barbecue. He has been featured in the *New York Times*, *National Geographic Traveler* magazine, *Bon Appétit*, and *Food & Wine*. He is also the founder of Barbecue University, headquartered at The Greenbrier resort in West Virginia. In 2003 he defeated Iron Chef Roksbura Michiba in a barbecue battle on Japanese television. He also has his own line of grilling tools, Best of Barbecue. His formal training was at Le Cordon Bleu and La Varenne cooking schools, Paris.

JIMMY SCHMIDT

THE RATTLESNAKE CLUB, DETROIT AND PALM SPRINGS

WWW.RATTLESNAKECLUB.COM

Native Midwesterner Jimmy Schmidt turned from electrical engineering to food after a trip to France. He attended two French culinary schools and later graduated first in his class at the Modern Gourmet in Newton, Massachusetts. He opened the first Rattlesnake Club in Denver, followed by Detroit, and in 2002 he opened The Rattlesnake Club in Palm Springs in the new Trump 29 Casino. His restaurants have been rated by the Zagat Survey as one of "America's Top Restaurants" from 2000 to 2005. From 2001 to 2005, the *Detroit Free Press* gave The Rattlesnake Club its "Ten Top Tables" award, and from 1993 to 2005, he has consistently won the DiRoNA Award. Schmidt is also CEO of Functional Food Company which produces his Smart Chocolate bars.

LYDIA SHIRE

LOCKE-OBER AND EXCELSIOR, BOSTON

WWW.LOCKE-OBER.COM; WWW.EXCELSIORRESTAURANT.COM

Lydia Shire has been named "America's Best Chef Northeast" and "one of America's Top Five Chefs" by the James Beard Foundation; one of the "Top Ten Chefs in America" by *Food & Wine*; and is a recipient of Restaurants & Institutions's Ivy Award. She trained at Le Cordon Bleu Cooking School, London, and got her first job at Maison Robert, Boston. She worked in some of the city's finest establishments thereafter, including the Copley Plaza's Café Plaza, and The Parker House. She opened the landmark Seasons at the Bostonian Hotel, and later, the Four Seasons, Beverly Hills as executive chef—the first woman to hold this title—before coming back home to Boston to open her first restaurant, Biba.

FRANK STITT

HIGHLANDS BAR AND GRILL; BOTTEGA AND CAFÉ BOTTEGA;

AND CHEZ FONFON, BIRMINGHAM, ALABAMA

WWW.HIGHLANDSBARANDGRILL.COM; WWW.BOTTEGARESTAURANT.COM

Gourmet called Frank Stitt the "culinary king of Alabama" and noted, "when we dream about an American restaurant, it looks and smells a lot like Highlands Bar and Grill." *Bon Appétit* called him one of the culinary "Legends of the Decade" for the 1990s. Like many of his peers, his move to the culinary world was not in his original plans. While studying philosophy at Berkeley in the 1970s, he met Alice Waters of Chez Panisse. She, along with Simca Beck and Richard Olney, became his mentors. He opened the Highlands Bar and Grill in 1982, where he merged French technique and sensibility with authentic Southern flavors.

TROY THOMPSON

JER-NE RESTAURANT + BAR AT THE RITZ CARLTON, MARINA DEL REY, CALIFORNIA
WWW.RITZCARLTON.COM/HOTELS/MARINA_DEL_REY/DINING/VENUES/JERNE_MARINA/
DEFAULT.HTML

Multi-award winning chef Troy Thompson defines umami as "deliciousness"—this from a man whose first food work began in a submarine sandwich shop. He trained under chef Hiroshi Noguchi in Chicago and then went on to train under Michelin Chef Gunther Seeger at the Ritz-Carlton, Buckhead (Atlanta). He then worked in Osaka, Japan, where he owned Remington's, an American cuisine restaurant. When he returned to the United States, he opened Fusebox in Atlanta, wininng praise from the start. Notably, Troy has twice hosted the Umami Dinner to benefit the Friends of James Beard, featuring tasting menus prepared by some of the world's great chefs.

RICK TRAMONTO

TRU AND OSTERIA VIA STATO, CHICAGO
WWW.TRAMONTOCUISINE.COM

Rick Tramonto has worked with some of the world's greatest chefs, including Pierre Gagnaire, Anton Mosimann, and Raymond Blanc. And to think, this culinary master described as a "magician in the kitchen" once flipped burgers at Wendy's. His first professional culinary experience came under Chef Greg Broman at the Strathallen Hotel in Rochester, New York. His first restaurant with Gale Gand was Trio; others that followed were Brasserie T, the Vanilla Bean Bakery, and in 1999 came Tru. Tru is a Mobil Four-Star restaurant, a Relais-Gourmand property, and an AAA Five Diamond restaurant, and Tramonto has received numerous awards as well, including the 2003 Ivy Award.

MING TSAI

BLUE GINGER, WELLESLEY, MA
WWW.MING.COM

As a young boy Ming Tsai cooked alongside his parents at the family's restaurant in Dayton, Ohio. He received a degree from Yale in mechanical engineering, but the summer he spent at Le Cordon Bleu, Paris, turned him back to food. He trained under renowned pastry chef Pierre Hermé in Paris, and then in Osaka with sushi master Kobayashi, and went on to graduate school at Cornell for his master's degree in hotel administration and hospitality marketing. He settled in Massachusetts and opened Blue Ginger with his wife, Polly. He has received kudos from the James Beard Foundation, *Esquire* Magazine, and the Zagat Restaurant Guide. He currently hosts Public Television's cooking show, Simply Ming, and has his own line of cookware and ingredients.

ANTHONY UGLESICH

UGLESICH'S, NEW ORLEANS

Anthony Uglesich's father Sam founded a seafood restaurant in New Orleans in the late 1920s, and Anthony worked there as a teenager along with other family members. He met his future wife, Gail Flettrich, in the 1960s, and by 1974, after his dad passed away, the business became theirs. They experimented and developed new dishes all along the way, and over the years, their little seafood dive in a not-so-great neighborhood has gained a massive following and much-deserved fame through stellar reviews. As of this writing, Uglesich's is scheduled to close soon, and the long lines of eager diners winding around the block waiting for seats will likely disappear.

NORMAN VAN AKEN

NORMAN'S, MIAMI
WWW.NORMANS.COM

Norman Van Aken started as a short order cook in diners in his native Illinois. A casual trip with some friends to the Florida Keys forever changed his life. It was there that he first took a serious restaurant job, setting in motion his climb from line cook to one of the premier chefs in the country. *The New York Times* honored Norman with the distinction of the best chef and best restaurant in South Florida, and Norman's was rated number one in food, service, and popularity for two consecutive years. *Food & Wine*, *Travel & Leisure*, *Bon Appétit*, and Condé Nast *Traveler* all have praised him. His awards include the Robert Mondavi Culinary Award of Excellence, Food Arts Silver Spoon for Lifetime Achievement, James Beard Foundation's Best Chef, Southeast. He has been called "father of New World Cuisine."

ALAN WONG

ALAN WONG'S RESTAURANT AND THE PINEAPPLE ROOM, HONOLULU
ALAN WONG'S HAWAII, JAPAN
WWW.ALANWONGS.COM

Alan Wong began his cooking career as an apprentice at The Greenbrier Hotel, and from there moved to Lutèce in New York City. His mentor, Andre Soltner, who emphasized the importance of skilled craftsmanship, made his mark on Wong. During the course of his career, he opened The Canoe House Restaurant at the Mauna Lani Bay Hotel and Bungalows, Alan Wong's Restaurant, and The Pineapple Room by Alan Wong at Macy's, all in Hawaii. His restaurants have received top ratings in Zagat, Gault Millau, *Gourmet*, *Bon Appétit* and *Food & Wine*. A three-time award winner from DiRoNA, he was inducted into the Fine Dining Hall of Fame by *Nation's Restaurant News*, and in 2002 was one of ten U.S. chefs nominated by the inaugural Wedgewood Awards for the title of World Master of Culinary Arts.

SOURCES

ASIAN FOODS

www.asianfoodgrocer.com, 1-877-360-1855

www.Asianawest.com

www.morethangourmet.com, 1-800-860-9385

www.templeofthai.com

www.importfood.com

www.pacificeastwest.com

CANE SYRUP

www.steensyrup.com

CEDAR PLANKS

www.barbeque-store.com

www.justsmokedsalmon.com/planks.htm

HERBS

www.glenbrookfarm.com

www.mountainroseherbs.com

www.earthmedicine.ca

www.linglesherbs.com

www.mulberrycreek.com

HUITLACOCHE (CUITLACOCHE)

Fresh and Wild, 1-360-737-3652

www.earthy.com, 1-800-367-4709

www.mexgrocer.com

www.gourmetsleuth.com

MEATS: KUROBUTA PORK; PREMIUM, ORGANIC, AND ARTISANAL BEEF, LAMB, VEAL, TURKEY, AND POULTRY

www.lobels.com

www.snakeriverfarms.com

www.dakotabeefcompany.com

www.greatwestcattle.com

www.montanalegend.com

www.lgbeef.com

MULTI-ETHNIC FOOD SOURCES, MAJOR WORLD CUISINES, FRESH AND PACKAGED

www.thecmccompany.com

www.seasonedpioneers.com

www.chefshop.com, 1-877-337-2491

www.quickspice.com

www.earthy.com, 1-800-367-4709

www.wildfoods.ca

www.glenbrookfarm.com, 1-888-716-7627

www.thespiceshop.co.uk

OAK LOGS AND WINE BARREL STAVES

www.barbecuebible.com

ORGANIC GROCERIES

www.greenearthorganics.com

www.diamondorganics.com

www.localharvest.com

www.villageorganics.com

www.organickitchen.com

www.outdoororganics.com

SHELLFISH, SUSHI FISH, UNI

P&J Oyster Company, 1-888-LA-BAYOU

www.thefreshlobstercompany.com

www.catalinaop.com

www.bcseafoodonline.com

SHISO SEEDS

www.gardenguides.com

SPROUT KITS; RARE AND FLOWERING EDIBLE PLANTS

www.sprouthouse.com

www.sacredseed.com

www.cameron.com

SUSHI RICE

www.kumaiharvest.com, 1-800-541-2233

BIBLIOGRAPHY

Akihiro, Furudate. "Free Amino Acids in Potato Tubers and Their Extraction by Boiling Water." *Journal of Home Economics of Japan* 52.1 (2001): 71–74.

Art Culinaire. "Umami: the Fifth Element—Fifth Element of Taste." Summer 2003.

Bachmanov, Alexander, Monell Chemical Senses Center. Telephone interview, January 4, 2005.

Bachmanov, Alexander, and Beauchamp, Gary K., "Genetics of Intake of Umami-tasting Solutions by Mice," *Sensory Neuron* 3.3 (2001): 205–212.

Bachmanov, Alexander, G. Michael Tordoff, and Gary K. Beachamp. *Basic Characteristics of Glutamates and Umami Sensing in the Oral Cavity and Gut, Intake of Umami-Tasting Solutions by Mice: A Genetic Analysis.* Presented at the International Symposium on Glutamate. October 12–14, 1998. Bergamo, Italy.

Barham, Peter. *The Science of Cooking.* New York: Springer, 2001.

Beauchamp, Gary K., and Paul Pearson. "Human Development and Umami Taste." *Physiology and Behavior* 49 (1991): 1009–1012.

Beauchamp, Gary K., Monell Chemical Senses Center. Telephone interview. January 5, 2005.

Beksan, E., et al. "Synthesis and Sensory Characterization of Novel Umami-Tasting Glutamate Glycoconjugates." *Journal of Agricultural Food Chemistry* 51.18 (2003): 5428-5436.

Bergeron, Vic. *Trader Vic's Pacific Island Cookbook.* New York: Doubleday and Company, Inc., 1968.

Brand, Joseph G. "Receptor and Transduction Processes for Umami Taste." *Journal of Nutrition* 130 (2000) 942S–945S.

Brillat-Savarin, Jean Anthelme. *The Physiology of Taste,* English translation of *La Physiologie du goût* (1825). New York: Liveright Publishing Corporation, 1948 edition.

Broihier, Catherine, rep Ajinomoto. Telephone interview, May 6 2005.

Cambero, Isabel M., et al. "Beef Broth Flavour: Relation of Components with the Flavor Developed at Different Cooking Temperatures." *Journal of the Science of Food and Agriculture* 80.10 (2000): 1519–1528.

Caparoso, Randal. Changing Wine Into Umami. Accessed January 14, 2005 at http://inetours.com/PagesWT/Pairing/Wine_Into_Umami.html.

Corriher, Shirley O. *CookWise, The Hows & Whys of Successful Cooking.* New York: William Morrow, 1997.

Dornenburg, Andrew, and Karen Page. *Culinary Artistry.* New York: Van Nostrand Reinhold, 1996.

DuBois, Grant E. "Unraveling the Biochemistry of Sweet and Umami Tastes." *Proceedings of the National Academy of Sciences in the United States* 101.39 (2004): 13972–13973.

EAFUS: A Food Additive Database, U.S. Department of Health and Human Services, U.S. Food and Drug Administration. Accessed April 15, 2005 at http://vm.cfsan.fda.gov/~dms/eafus.html.

Engel, Karl Heinz, Irwin Hornstein, and Roy Teranishi, eds. "Special Issue on Umami." *Food Reviews International* 14.2&3 (1998): 123–338.

"FDA and Monosodium Glutamate." August 31, 1995. U.S. Department of Health and Human Services, U.S. Food and Drug Administration. Accessed January 12, 2005 at http://vm.cfsan.fda.gov/~lrd/msg.html.

Fernstrom, John D. "Second International Conference on Glutamate: Conference Summary." *Journal of Nutrition* 130 (2000): 1077S–1079S.

Goral, Dan. Sokol and Company. Telephone interview, February 25, 2005.

Gugino, Sam. "Umami, the Fifth Taste." *Wine Spectator.* May 31, 2003.

Halpern, Bruce P. "Glutamate and the Flavor of Foods." *Journal of Nutrition* 130 (2000): 910S–914S.

Hegenbart, Scott. "Filtering the Facts on Flavor Enhancers." *Food Product Design.* February 1994.

———. "Flavor Enhancement: Making the Most of What's There." *Food Product Design.* February 1992.

Honing In on a Receptor for the Fifth Taste. February 25, 2002. Howard Hughes Medical Institute. Accessed March 2, 2005 at http://www.hhmi.org/news/zuker3.html.

Hwang, Deng-Fwu, et al. "Seasonal Variations of Free Amino Acids and Nucleotide-Related Compounds in the Muscle of Cultured Taiwanese Puffer Takifugi Rubripes." *Fisheries Science* 66.6 (2000): 1123.

IFIC Review on Monosodium Glutamate: Examining the Myths. November, 2001. *International Food Information Council Foundation.* Accessed May 8, 2005 at http://ific.org/publications/reviews/msgir.cfm.

Ikeda, Kukinae, PhD., "New Seasonings." *Journal of the Chemical Society of Japan* 30 (1909): 820–836.

International Congress of Applied Chemistry. *The Tech: Massachusetts Institute of Technology.* March 30 1911: 1.

Iseki, Keiko, et al. "Umami Taste: Electrophysiological Recordings of Synergism in Mouse Taste Cells." *Sensory Neuron* 3.3 (2001): 155–167.

Kapoor, Sybil. *Taste, a New Way to Cook.* North Vancouver, UK: Whitecap, 2003.

Kawai, Misako, Atsushi Okiyami, and Yoychi Ueda. "Taste Enhancements Between Various Amino Acids and IMP." *Chemical Senses* 27 (2002) 739–745.

Kemp, Sarah, and Gary K. Beauchamp. "Flavor Modification by Sodium Chloride and Monosodium Glutamate." *Journal of Food Science* 59.3 (1994): 682–686.

Kimeo, Iwano, et al. "Search for the Amino Acids Affecting the Taste of Japanese Sake." *Journal of the Brewing Society of Japan* 99.9 (2004): 659–664.

Kohmura, Masanori, et al., inventors. Process for producing a flavor-enhancing material for foods. U.S. Patent and Trademark Office, Patent Application #20040265471. Filed December 2, 2002.

Kokumi—the Subtle Key to Deeper Flavors. Kyowa Hakko Kogyo Co. Ltd., Tokyo. Accessed March 12, 2005 at http://www.kyowa.co.jp/eng/kankyoe/er2004e3.pdf.

Kulkarni, A.D., et al. "Influence of Dietary Nucleotide Restriction on Bacterial Sepsis and Phagocytic Cell Function in Mice." *Archives of Surgery* 121.2 (1986).

Kurihara, Kenzo, and Makato Kashiwayanagi. "Physiological Studies on Umami Taste." *Journal of Nutrition* 130 (2000): 931S–934S.

Kurlansky, Mark. *Salt, A World History.* New York: Walker and Company, 2002.

Kuroda, et al., inventors. Taste Enhancer, "Kokumi." United States Patent, 5,679,397. Filed 1995.

Lawless, H.T. "Flavor." In *Handbook of Perception and Cognition, Vol. 16, Cognitive Ecology.* E. C. Carterrette and M. P. Friedman, eds. San Diego: Academic Press, 1996. pp. 325–380.

Lin W, Ogura T, Kinnamon SC. "Responses to di-sodium guanosine 5'-monophospate and monosodium L-glutamate in taste receptor cells of rat fungiform papillae." *Journal of Physiology* (2005) 89: 1434–1439.

Lindemann, Bernd, Yoko Agiwara, and Yuzo Ninomiya. "The Discovery of Umami." *Chemical Senses* 27 (2002): 843–844.

Lindemann, Bernd. "A Taste for Umami." *Nature: Neuroscience* 3.2 (2000) 99–100.

Löliger, Jurg. "Function and Importance of Glutamate for Savory Foods." *Journal of Nutrition* 130 (2000): 915S–920S.

McGee, Harold. *On Food and Cooking, The Science and Lore of the Kitchen.* New York: Scribner, 2004.

McGregor, Richard. "Taste Modification in the Biotech Era." *Food Technology* 58.5 (2004): 24–30.

Mojet, Jos, E.P. Kostner, and J.F. Prinz. "Do Tastants Have a Smell?" *Chemical Senses* 30 (2005): 9–21.

Mojet, Jos, Johannes Heidema, and Elly Christ-Hazelhof. "Effect of Concentration on Taste-Taste Interaction in Foods for Elderly and Young Subjects." *Chemical Senses* 29 (2004): 671–681.

Mowbray, Scott. "Golf Life: A Yen for the High End." *Travel & Leisure* November 2004.

Nelson, Greg, et al. "An Amino Acid Taste Receptor." *Nature* 416 (2002): 199–202.

Ninomiya, K., ed. "Umami: A Universal Taste." *Food Reviews International* 18.1 (2002): 23–38.

Okiyama, Atsushi, and Gary K. Beauchamp. "Taste Dimensions of Monosodium Glutamate in a Food System: Role of Glutamate in Young American Subjects." *Physiology and Behavior* 65.1 (1998) 177–181.

Prescott, John, and Ariane Young. "Does Information about MSG (Monosodium Glutamate) Content Influence Consumer Ratings of Soups With and Without MSG?" *Appetite* 39 (2002): 25–33.

Pszczola, Donald E. "Dawning of the Age of Proteins." *Food Technology* 58.2 (2004) 56–69.

———. "Flavor Enhancement: Taking Off the Mask." *Food Technology* 58.8 (2004) 56–69.

————. "The Changing Perception of Taste Perception." *Food Technology* 58.11 (2004) 56–71.

"Researchers Define Molecular Basis of Human 'Sweet Tooth' and Umami Taste." November 4, 2003. The Human Molecular Genetics Portal Site. Accessed March 3, 2005 at http://hum-molgen.org/NewsGen/11-2003/msg11.html.

Robuchon, Joël, et al. *Larousse Gastronomique.* New York: Clarkson Potter, 2001.

Rolls, Edwin T. "The Representation of Umami Taste in the Taste Cortex." *Journal of Nutrition* 130 (2000) 960S–965S.

Rouhi, A. Maureen. "Unlocking the Secrets of Taste." *Chemical and Engineering World* September 10, 2001: 42–46.

Sako, Noritaka, et al. "Synergistic Responses of the Chroda Tympani to Mixtures of Umami and Sweet Substances in Rats." *Chemical Senses* 28 (2002): 261–266.

Samuels, Jack L. "MSG Dangers and Deceptions." Price Potenger Nutrition Foundation 1997–2000. Accessed May 25, 2004 at http://www.price-pottenger.org/Articles/MSG.html.

Schiffman, Susan S. "Intensification of Sensory Properties of Foods for the Elderly." *Journal of Nutrition* 130 (2000): 927S–930S.

Smith, David V., and Robert F. Margolski. "Making Sense of Taste." *Scientific American* March 18, 2001.

Steingarten, Jeffrey. *It Must've Been Something I Ate.* New York: Vintage Books, 2002.

Taste of Amino Acids. Amino Acid Department, AminoScience Division, Ajinomoto Co., Inc., Tokyo. Accessed March 15, 2005 at http://www.ajinomoto.co.jp/amino/e_aminoscience/bc/b-7.html.

Tokiko, Mizuno, and Yamada Koji. "Change in the Free Amino Acid Composition of Soybeans by Soaking in Water." *Journal of Home Economics of Japan* 53.12 (2002): 1197–1202.

"Umami in Molecular Gastronomy." Beauchamp, Gary, Heston Blumenthal, Nobuyuki Matsuhisa, Yoshihiro Murata, Edmund T. Rolls, Yasuhiro Sasajima, and Kathy Sykes. International Glutamate Information Service, London, 2004.

USDA Nutrient Database for Standard Reference Release 17. U.S. Department of Agriculture Nutrient Data Laboratory, 2004.

Walker, R. "The Significance of Excursions Above the ADI. Case Study: Monosodium Glutamate." *New England Journal of Medicine* 30 (2 pt 2) (Oct 1999): 199S–121S.

Wolke, Robert L. *What Einstein Told His Cook.* New York: Norton, 2003.

————. *What Einstein Told His Cook 2.* New York: Norton, 2005.

www.monell.org. The Monell Chemical Senses Center, 3500 Market St., Philadelphia, PA.

www.srut.org. Society for Research on Umami Taste, Japan.

Yamaguchi, Shizuko, and Kumiko Ninomiya. "Umami and Food Palatability." *Journal of Nutrition* 130 (2000): 921S–926S.

Zhao, Grace Q., et al. "The Receptors for Mammalian Sweet and Umami Taste." *Cell* 115.3 (2003): 255–266.

ACKNOWLEDGMENTS

First, our thanks to Chris Steighner, our editor, for believing from the start that umami's time has come. Thanks to each of the chefs whose umami recipes are the essence of this book. Many thanks to the chefs' support staffs who sweated the details that really make a book happen.

Thanks to Mark Bittman, author of *How to Cook Everything*, for his interest in spreading the word about umami, and for his contribution of the foreword.

Special thanks to Dr. Gary Beauchamp and Alexander Bachmanov of The Monell Chemical Senses Center, Philadelphia, for their insights and knowledge, and to Leslie Stein for putting us in touch with them. Also our thanks to Kumiko Ninomiya, Sumio Aoki, Catherine Broihier, and Brenden Naulty of the Ajinomoto Company for the essential facts and research they generously provided. Also to Dan Gorel of Sokol and Company for his perspective on the true nature of umami. Thanks to Robert L. Wolke for his sharp eye and valuable guidance on matters of scientific accuracy. And to Chefs Shirley Cheng, David Kamen, Michael Pardus, and Jonathan Zearfoss of the Culinary Institute of America for the guidance and inestimable knowledge that they graciously shared.

And finally, as always, we want our families to know we are alive and well, and yes, ready for the next umami cookbook.

RECIPE CREDITS

Sea Scallops with Mashed Potatoes and Red Onion Confit adapted from *Cooking with Daniel Boulud*, Random House © 1993.

Short Ribs Braised in Red Wine with Celery Duo adapted from *Daniel Boulud's Café Boulud Cookbook*, by Daniel Boulud and Dorie Greenspan, Scribner © 1999.

Lamb Shanks with Tomatoes and Oyster Stew with Dry Sherry adapted from *The Cook's Bible*, Little, Brown and Company © 1996, with permission from Christopher Kimball.

Spicy Sour Botan Shrimp and Cilantro Soup with Monkfish adapted from *Nobu, the Cookbook*, Kondansha International © 2001 by Nobuyuki Matsuhisa.

Original versions of Marinated Skirt Steak with Avocado-Tomatillo Dipping Sauce and Huitlacoche Quesadillas © Mary Sue Milliken and Susan Feniger.

Green Bean Tempura with Asian Dipping Sauce and Fire and Ice: Seared Peppered Tuna with Daikon Radish and Cucuber Sorbet adapted from *Patrick O'Connell's Refined American Cuisine: The Inn at Little Washington*, by Patrick O'Connell, Bulfinch © 2004.

Anchoyade-Grilled Cedar-Planked Bluefish or Salmon adapted from *Steven Raichlen's BBQ USA* by Steven Raichlen, Workman Publishing © 2005.

Wood-Grilled Rib Steak with Shiitake-Wine Sauce adapted from *Raichlen's Indoor! Grilling*, by Steven Raichlen, Workman Publishing © 2005.

Portobello and Chanterelle Mushroom Cylinder and Vanilla-Scented Lobster with Asparagus Thread Salad © Jimmy Schmidt - Rattlesnake.

Red Snapper with Ham Hock-Red Wine Sauce and Pea Cakes with Tomato Salsa excerpted from *Frank Stitt's Southern Table*, © by Frank Stitt, used by permission of Artisan, a division of Workman Publishing Co., Inc., New York. All Rights Reserved.

Original version of Pan-Roasted Cumin-Rubbed Breast of Chicken with Plantain-Foie Gras "Mofongo" on My *Very* Black Bean Sauce from *Norman's New World Cuisine* by Norman Van Aken, Random House © 1997.

Unless otherwise noted, all recipes are copyrighted by their respective chefs.

CHEFS' PHOTO CREDITS

DANIEL BOULUD BY **BILL MILNE**

GARY DANKO BY **KINGMOND YOUNG**

HUBERT KELLER BY **JAMES GARRAHAN**

CHRISTOPHER KIMBALL BY **KELLER & KELLER**

NOBU MATSUHISA BY **STEVEN FREEMAN**

PATRICK O'CONNELL BY **SANDRO MILLER**

STEVEN RAICHLEN BY **FERNANDO DIAZ**

JIMMY SCHMIDT BY **LISA SPINDLER**

LYDIA SHIRE BY **DOM MIGUEL**

KEN ORINGER BY **BOBBY DIMARZO**

FRANK STITT BY **CHRISTOPHER HIRSHEIMER**

TROY THOMPSON BY **BRIAN KRAMMER**

RICK TRAMONTO BY **TIM TURNER**

MING TSAI BY **DARI MICHELE**

NORMAN VAN AKEN BY **YESIKKA VIVANCOS**

ALAN WONG BY **MARY ANN CHANGG**

All photos are copyrighted by the photographers listed above.

Page references in **boldface** refer to
illustrations.